(Chapter 1)

The days grew into darkness so fast. It seemed almost as if the sun set as soon as it had risen to Jimmy. There was never enough time in the day to get anything done. Always on a deadline and in a pinch. That was the life of the young man. Luck never seemed to roll his way. Not in the first 16 years of his life anyway for that matter.

All he had seem to experience at this point in his life were the ways of the wicked. The wars allover the world that never seemed to stop. The killing of the beautiful whales in the oceans. The fish as well as the dolphins and so on and so forth. So many other kinds of sea life. He'd seen the horrible sins of woman and man as well. The wrong doing of other human beings.

It really had changed his views on life. And what it really meant to be alive. Dog eat dog was the meaning of life. It had been taught to him from a child. And it was mostly what he'd witnessed to this point. The corruption of the entire world. So many different situations had been made apparent to him at such an early age in life. His father had taught him how to read through others from an early age.

He wanted to see the world change and for the better not the worst. He'd been told so many times before that the world had taken a turn for the worst. And it wouldn't be long before the Lord would come down and smite the sinners. And send the non believers to hell. And take his followers home, finally once and for all.

Jimmy didn't want to be part of the smitten. He now was a young man whom had become God fearing. Which for him was life changing and a very important moment. He would hope that the others in his hometown would follow him along his journey. As he would hopefully lead them down the path of straight and narrow. And on into a better way of living.

(Chapter 2)

Several things would take place that would change the whole aspect of how Jimmy looked at life. Not long after turning 18 he would lose a couple close friends to horrible accidents. Sending him spiraling out of control. With no end in sight or so it seemed to be the situation. Addiction would take over sooner or later. Digging it's claws into him good and deep.

This would start a series of events that would make life a living hell on Jimmy for many years to come. Drinking and partying would consume his life for a very long time. Life during this years would become very difficult. A marriage that would only last two years. Two children that would be kept away from him for well over twenty years along the way.

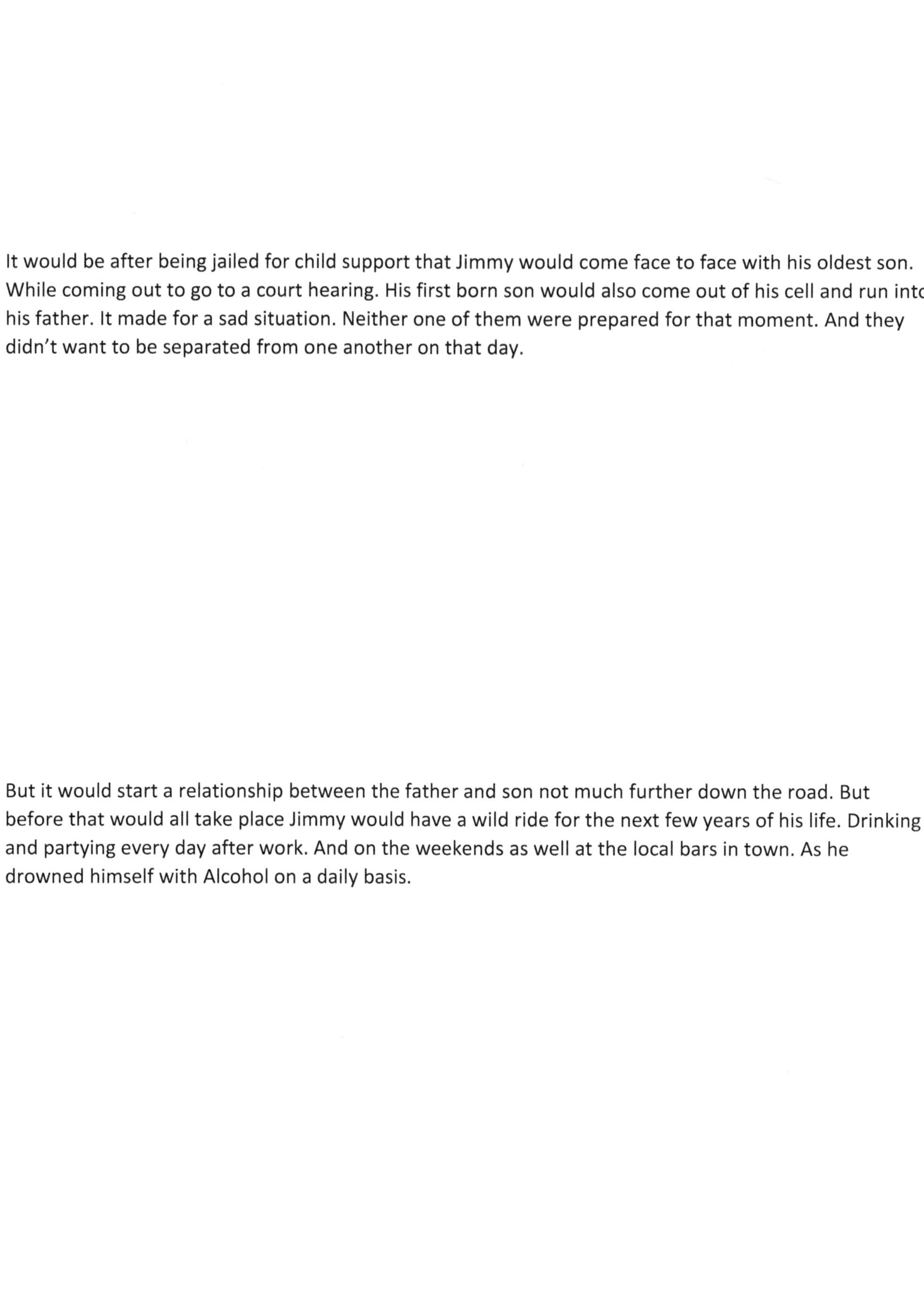

It would be after being jailed for child support that Jimmy would come face to face with his oldest son. While coming out to go to a court hearing. His first born son would also come out of his cell and run into his father. It made for a sad situation. Neither one of them were prepared for that moment. And they didn't want to be separated from one another on that day.

But it would start a relationship between the father and son not much further down the road. But before that would all take place Jimmy would have a wild ride for the next few years of his life. Drinking and partying every day after work. And on the weekends as well at the local bars in town. As he drowned himself with Alcohol on a daily basis.

And it was during these times that the Chaos and Mayhem would take place in his life. So many ups and downs, as well as tragedies would also take place. The death of his Aunt Brenda and his Grandfather Luke as well. Then the death of his Uncle Chris was a very emotional time for him. His Death had came as fast as ever. And it was clear to see that Jimmy wasn't ready for that at all.

(Chapter 3)

Chris had died so suddenly at a young age. They said it was Leukemia that had taken his life. And, the Cancer didn't take long to do the job. It felt as if he were taken from them overnight. The funeral was soon after prepared so quickly. Noone had time to really mourn the process at all. He went out In style though and, that was all that really mattered to Jimmy.

His life had been total hell up to this point. He wanted a way out from all of the pain he was feeling. Death was just to much for him to handle. After all it wasn't just one death he'd experienced. It was one

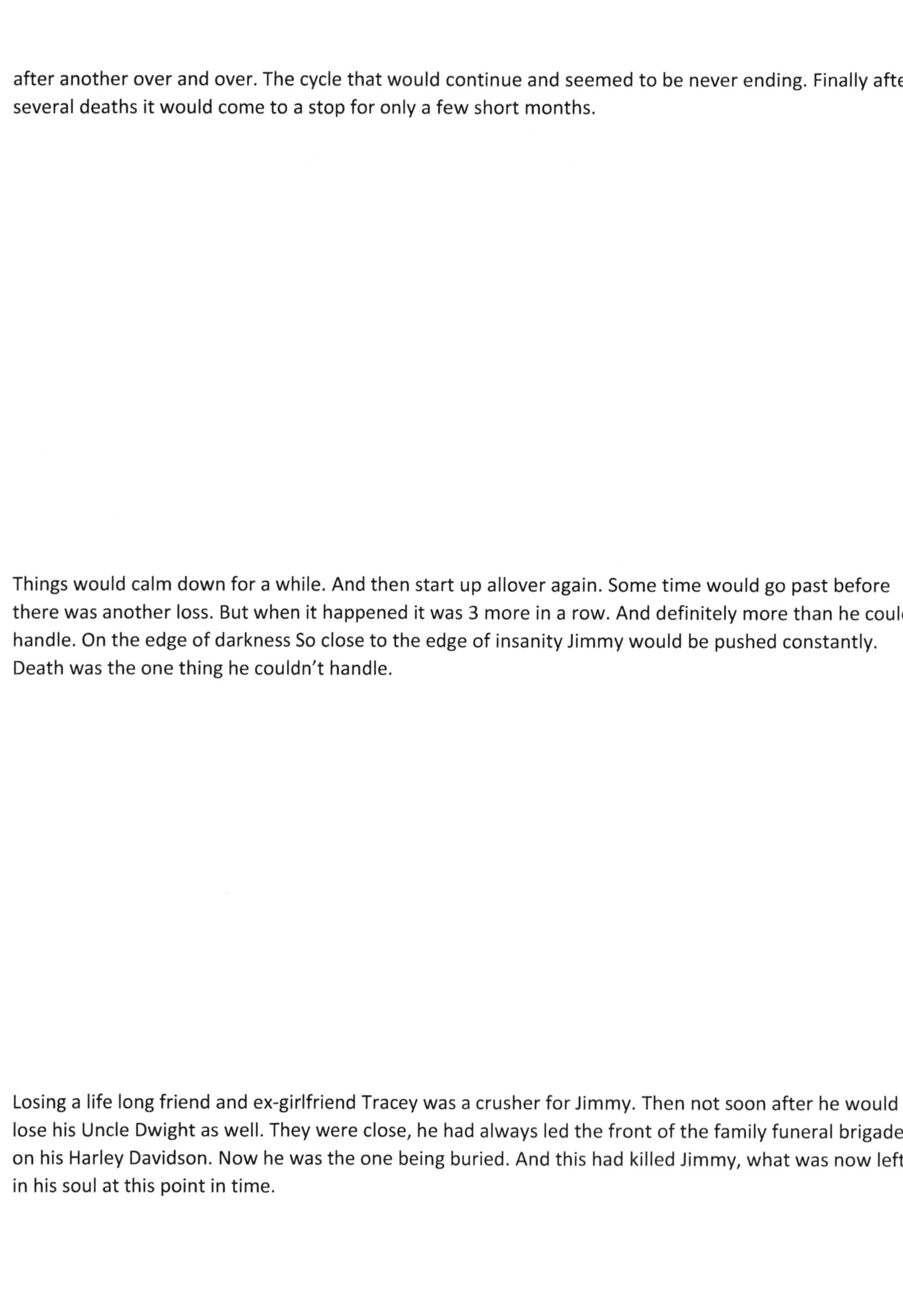

after another over and over. The cycle that would continue and seemed to be never ending. Finally after several deaths it would come to a stop for only a few short months.

Things would calm down for a while. And then start up allover again. Some time would go past before there was another loss. But when it happened it was 3 more in a row. And definitely more than he could handle. On the edge of darkness So close to the edge of insanity Jimmy would be pushed constantly. Death was the one thing he couldn't handle.

Losing a life long friend and ex-girlfriend Tracey was a crusher for Jimmy. Then not soon after he would lose his Uncle Dwight as well. They were close, he had always led the front of the family funeral brigades on his Harley Davidson. Now he was the one being buried. And this had killed Jimmy, what was now left in his soul at this point in time.

Almost as soon as they buried Dwight their was another death almost instantly. And this ruined whatever may have been left inside of Jimmy and his soul. He battled with his sanity for a long time after that. The drinking the drugging would suppress and kill the pain he felt inside. After many years of this he would try to change the situation.

(Chapter 4)

He figured then after starting to become ill. That he would try to find love out of all things. All he would find out in that process was that he looked for it in all of the wrong places. Bars and parties allover his hometown he'd go to and hang out at. He knew very many people and they all pretty much lived the same way that he did.

Most often the wild times would take place as the darkness fell. The parties would start and the groups would gather together and do their nightly scampers about the town or towns that surrounded them all. From burning tires at the nearest river. To partying at a good friends house and jamming the stereo full blast. Even swimming at the river in the Black of darkness was always an option.

Some nights the use of hallucinogenic drugs would make their way into town. And the parties really got hot. Often the group would take the party to the river. To avoid getting arrested for being disorderly. Continuing all night long until the early hours of dawn. The watching of the Purple and Pink leaves swaying from the trees from left to right. All they would see were the outlines of the tree's.

The fire burning in every single shade of the color spectrum. Life was lived this way for many years with Jimmy. Just trying to numb the pain of the world before it had reached anywhere near his soul again. The next few years would be filled with sickness and torment. Jimmy pressed on still looking for love in all of the wrong places. Every single weekend for years on end.

By the age of 26 Jimmy had already conceived not one or two. But 5 boys of his own. And was now working at a local paper mill on the out skirts of town. 6 days a week he'd work sometimes. Recycling paper for a greener earth. It was his calling, Or so he had thought. So he gladly had accepted the job offer. After a few years he became the plant manager. As he now found himself running the entire plant.

(Chapter 5)

Working very long hours on most days of the week. He wouldn't have much time to himself at all. When there was time it was mostly spent on drinking and playing softball to keep his pain at bay. When he wasn't doing those two things. He would be fishing or camping to find that inner peace once again. While camping out at a section of the woods by the Miami River.

Jimmy had spent most of his childhood years in the woods. And almost every weekend in the forest as an adult as well. He loved the woods. It was Jimmie's Sanctuary. His safe haven his peace of mind. He found energy there to keep pushing forward in life. And it had managed to work for a very long time for him. That was the only place where Jimmy could think clearly.

After work on so many days he would leave and head straight for the gravel pits. To fish and be at peace. Before going home to his wife and children. He had just become a married man and a father as well. Both of the combined situations. Had taken his mental status to hell almost immediately one after the other.

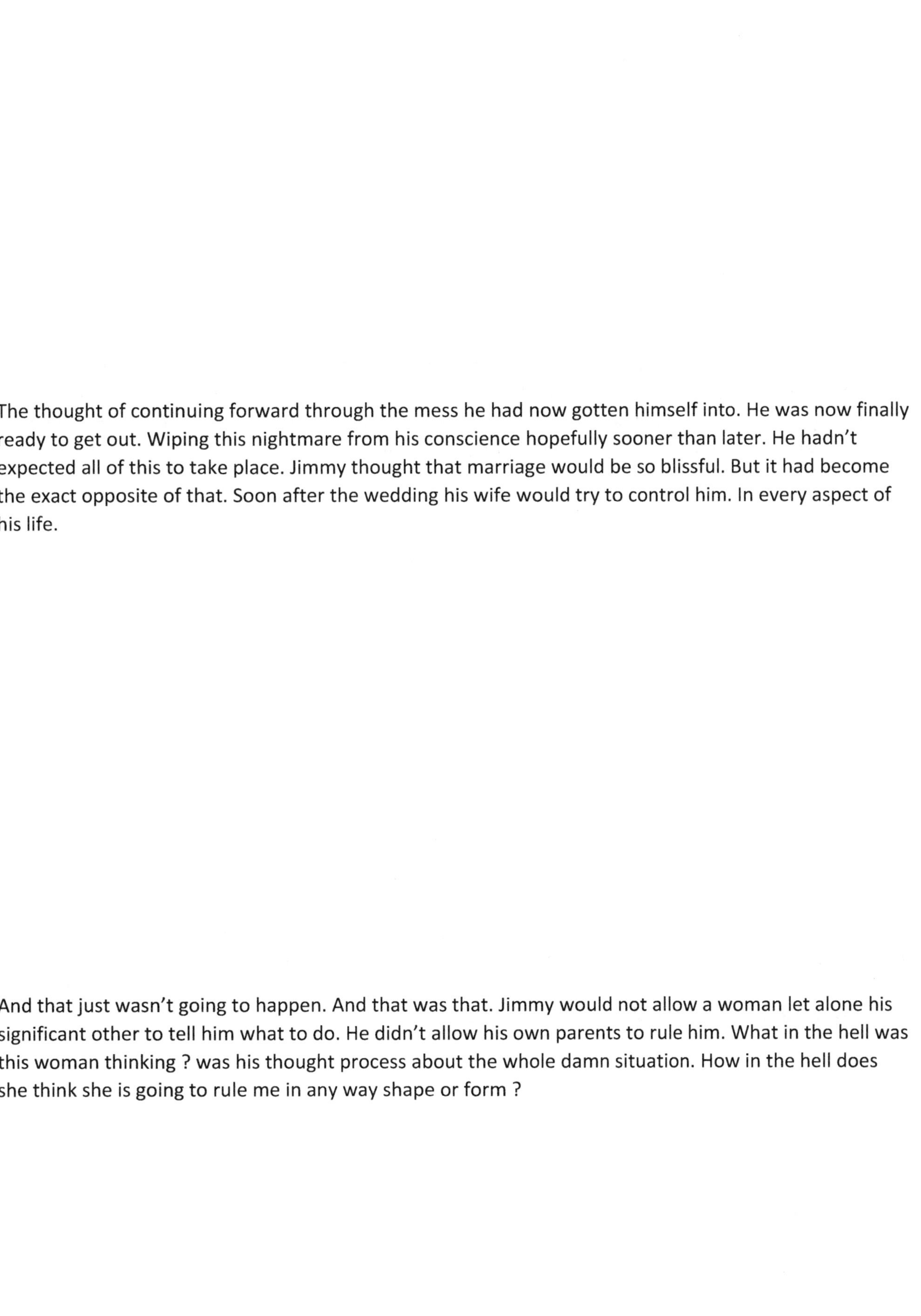

The thought of continuing forward through the mess he had now gotten himself into. He was now finally ready to get out. Wiping this nightmare from his conscience hopefully sooner than later. He hadn't expected all of this to take place. Jimmy thought that marriage would be so blissful. But it had become the exact opposite of that. Soon after the wedding his wife would try to control him. In every aspect of his life.

And that just wasn't going to happen. And that was that. Jimmy would not allow a woman let alone his significant other to tell him what to do. He didn't allow his own parents to rule him. What in the hell was this woman thinking ? was his thought process about the whole damn situation. How in the hell does she think she is going to rule me in any way shape or form ?

(Chapter 6)

That was all he could take. That was the moment that he had decided whether to stay in the marriage. Or if it were time to file for a divorce. He had learned over the years that he wasn't happy at all with this woman anymore. In fact he had been miserable for well over a couple of years now. Time had worn on him drastically. The control had ruined the marriage in all aspects.

He knew right then and there that it was time to call a lawyer and actually get the ball rolling. To file for a divorce and try to get visitation of his boy's. If his soon to be ex wife wouldn't deprive him of seeing his own children. He thought that it was very likely possible. She had been acting way out side of her personality lately. Almost as if she had been broken.

She had just started going back to school. Going back to a little small town College. Located in the City of Blue ash Ohio. And soon after everything about her would change. In just after a few short weeks. She would start to sleep with her pants on for no apparent reason. And he was thinking that an affair had been likely possible. He felt it in his gut. Something was way off about her as of late.

He had to get out of this partnership that was a one sided deal to him. He worked two jobs and then came home everyday soon after clocking out. Then after arriving home and eating his dinner. Once after that had been done. He would spend time with his two sons. Then not long after that, It was time for bed once again. And then after 8 hours of sleep. It was time to head off to work the next day.

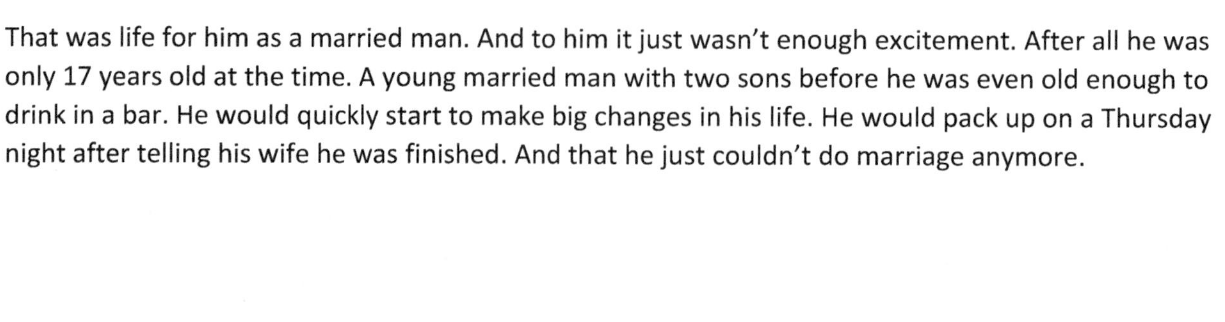

That was life for him as a married man. And to him it just wasn't enough excitement. After all he was only 17 years old at the time. A young married man with two sons before he was even old enough to drink in a bar. He would quickly start to make big changes in his life. He would pack up on a Thursday night after telling his wife he was finished. And that he just couldn't do marriage anymore.

(Chapter 7)

He had already covered his tracks earlier that week. On a Monday he had contacted a friend of his Aunt Brenda's. Asking them if they had a room for rent. In fact they did have a room for rent. But only for him they had said to the young man. They had received a phone call from his Aunt Brenda. On a Sunday evening. And she had asked them for a small favor.

They continued to tell the young man. How his Aunt had pleaded with them that it was much needed. And that he had just separated from his wife. And had needed an apartment as soon as possible. So it was agreed to allow him to move in. Jimmy had went in and paid the landlord two months rent upon meeting them. Which made a great impression for the young man.

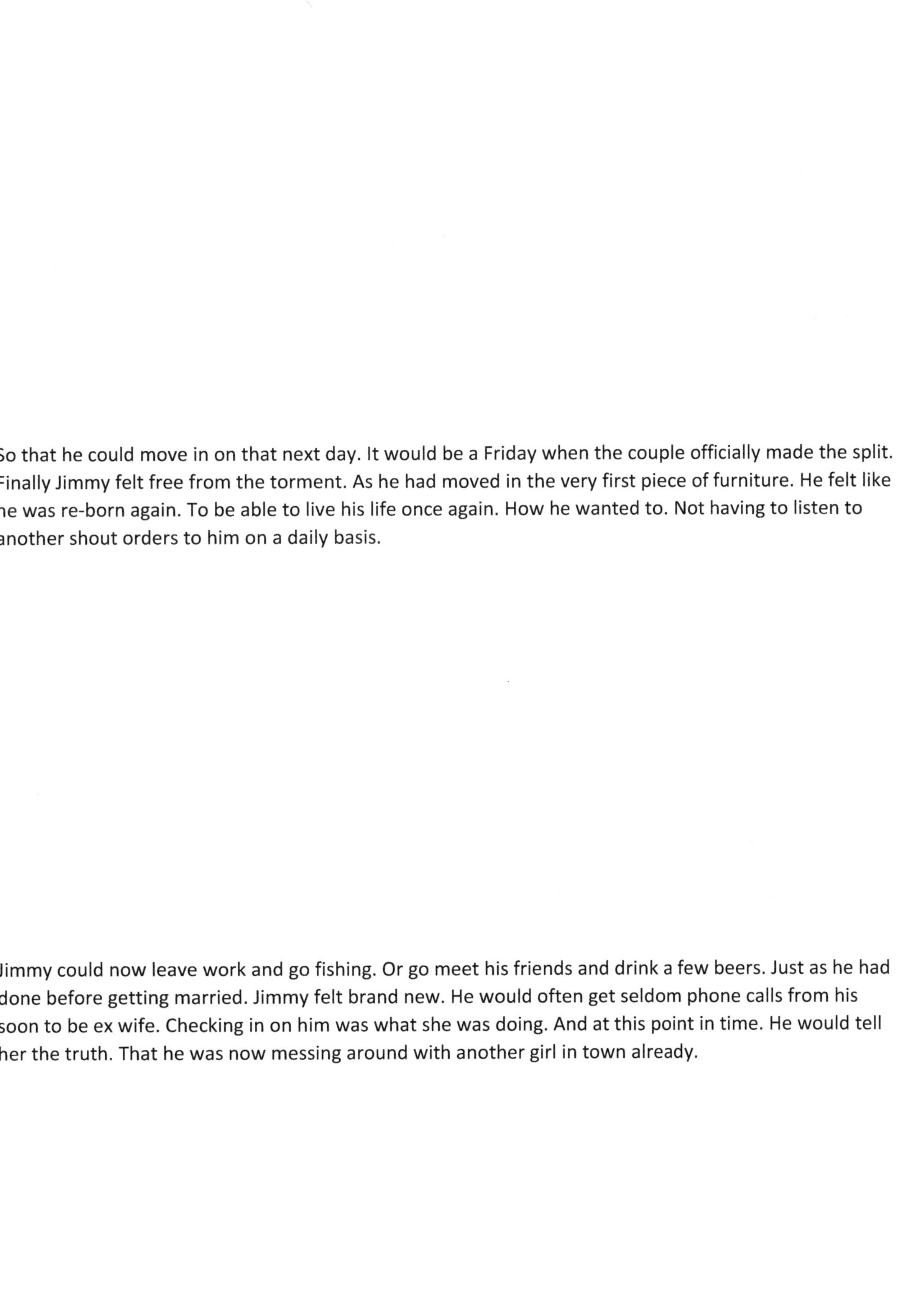

So that he could move in on that next day. It would be a Friday when the couple officially made the split. Finally Jimmy felt free from the torment. As he had moved in the very first piece of furniture. He felt like he was re-born again. To be able to live his life once again. How he wanted to. Not having to listen to another shout orders to him on a daily basis.

Jimmy could now leave work and go fishing. Or go meet his friends and drink a few beers. Just as he had done before getting married. Jimmy felt brand new. He would often get seldom phone calls from his soon to be ex wife. Checking in on him was what she was doing. And at this point in time. He would tell her the truth. That he was now messing around with another girl in town already.

The wife would not he very happy. She would soon blow up over the phone. Calling him every curse word in the book. Jimmy then just simply hung up on her and, un plugged the phone from the wall. He'd gone through this so many times before. Constantly being accused of cheating on her. So it was really simple for him in all honesty. Jimmy knew exactly why she was acting that way.

(Chapter 8)

Jimmy had already caught her Red handed in the act of cheating. He had came home from work one day early. And decided to soak in the bath tub. Something had told him to open the medicine cabinet. And when he did he would finally see why he had been accused so many times of cheating. Jimmy suddenly found himself looking at two different bottles of Antibiotics.

Jimmy now got out of the bath tub and had an idea come to him in that moment. He decided to call the Norwood Health Department. A nurse answered the phone and Jimmy asked her a question. The question was what were two separate bottles of Antibiotics used for. The Nurse replied quickly back to him. Informing him that he may need to get treated.

She stated that they would both be used to treat a known Sexually Transmitted Disease. That was the moment that had really ended the marriage between Jimmy and his wife. He now knew why she had acted a fool for so long. And that he could finally come to terms with the whole damn thing. That was when he decided to get a new apartment for himself.

.After the furniture had all been moved in it was still early on a Friday night. Jimmy would be ready to go out and party a little bit. It was still way to early to go to bed. The night was still very young. He decided to get dressed up and head over to Diane's house. She was like a second mother to me he had thought in that moment. And Angel was there he knew that for a fact to be sure.

Jimmy made the drive over to the other side of town. And had arrived at Diane's house. He got out and walked up to the door and knocked. Bud had came and answered the door. He greeted Jimmy as they both walked into the kitchen. Diane and several others were playing Spades at the time. Jimmy said he wanted to get in and play after that game was over.

(Chapter 9)

The game had finished and Jimmy picked Angel as his partner and the two of them sat down at the table. The next few hours would be spent playing cards and flirting very heavily were Jimmy and Angel. They would end up winning the first game. And after they had finished everyone went into the living room. To relax and unwind for a little while.

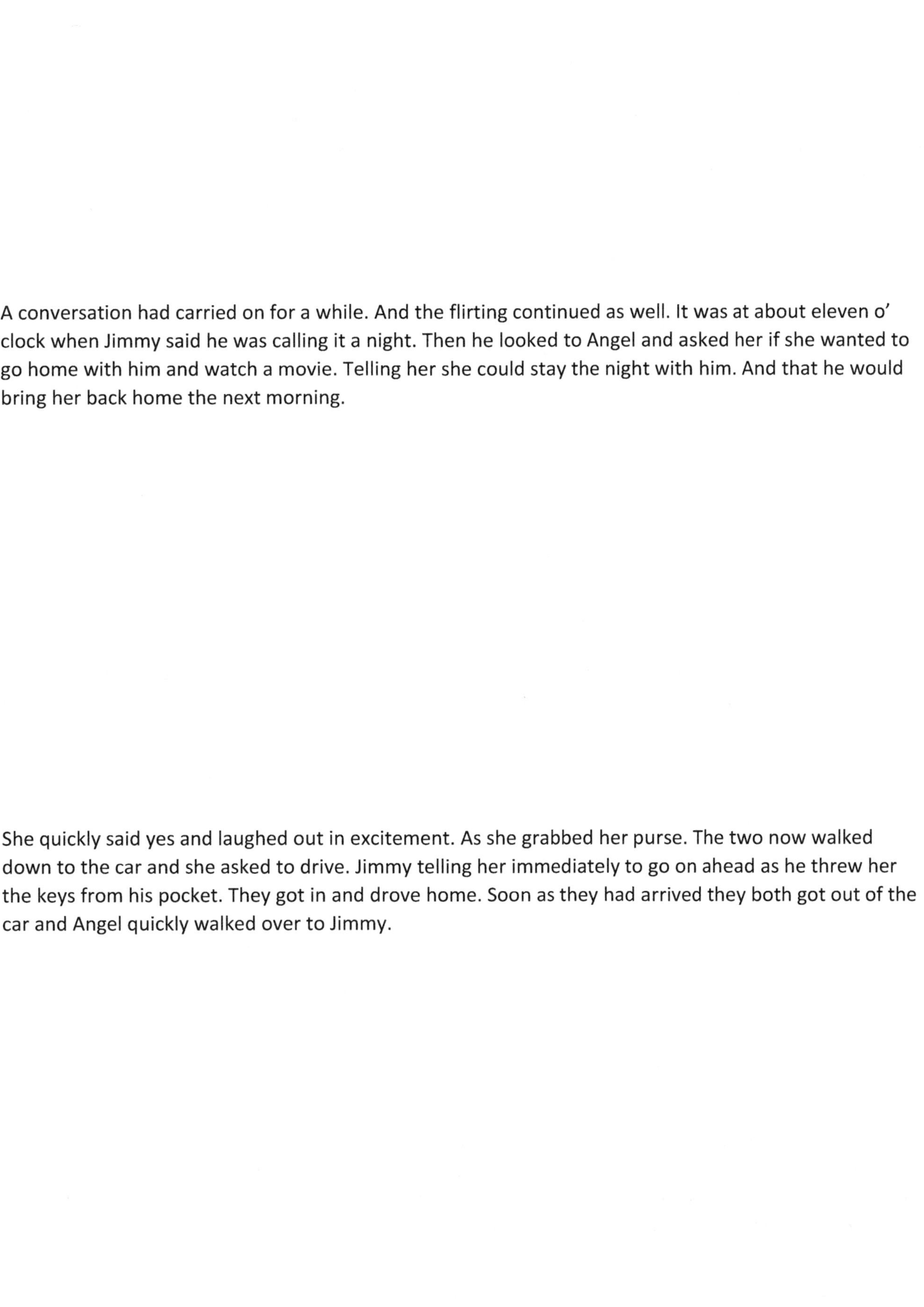

A conversation had carried on for a while. And the flirting continued as well. It was at about eleven o' clock when Jimmy said he was calling it a night. Then he looked to Angel and asked her if she wanted to go home with him and watch a movie. Telling her she could stay the night with him. And that he would bring her back home the next morning.

She quickly said yes and laughed out in excitement. As she grabbed her purse. The two now walked down to the car and she asked to drive. Jimmy telling her immediately to go on ahead as he threw her the keys from his pocket. They got in and drove home. Soon as they had arrived they both got out of the car and Angel quickly walked over to Jimmy.

She got close to him and started to lean forward as their lips met and they started to kiss. Jimmy now had a bit of fear come to him in that moment. Hoping his wife wasn't around sitting there watching him. He knew what she was capable of. And knew she was most likely sitting there somewhere. He told Angel to come in quickly with him.

The two new love birds were upstairs and inside of the house now. As they took off their clothes and got ready for bed. Angel walked off for the bathroom first. In order to freshen herself up just a bit. Jimmy now jumped into bed. Excited like a young child who was waiting on Santa clause to come. Angel came walking back in and slid into the bed so gracefully.

She then said to Jimmy I've waited on this moment for a lifetime. Do you even have a clue that I have always liked you ? Jimmy started to kiss her deeply now as they joined together expressing their passion for each other. Jimmy took control but was not over powering. As he now slid down the bed and his face now faced her thighs as he gently spread her legs apart.

(Chapter 10)

Jimmy now took his mouth and kissed her wetness excitingly. As he was now trying to make her want him madly. He continued for hours, caressing her lower body making her explode in Orgasm time and time again. The bed was now soaking wet from her passion. She now waited for Jimmy to take her with his fire. And he did so in many ways please her.

For hours the two new lovers made love. Time and time again. Allover the whole damn house they made love. On the counter tops on the love chair as well. Even on the kitchen sink and table they made love to one another. The new love he was now feeling was so exciting. They would continue to see each other for the next few months.

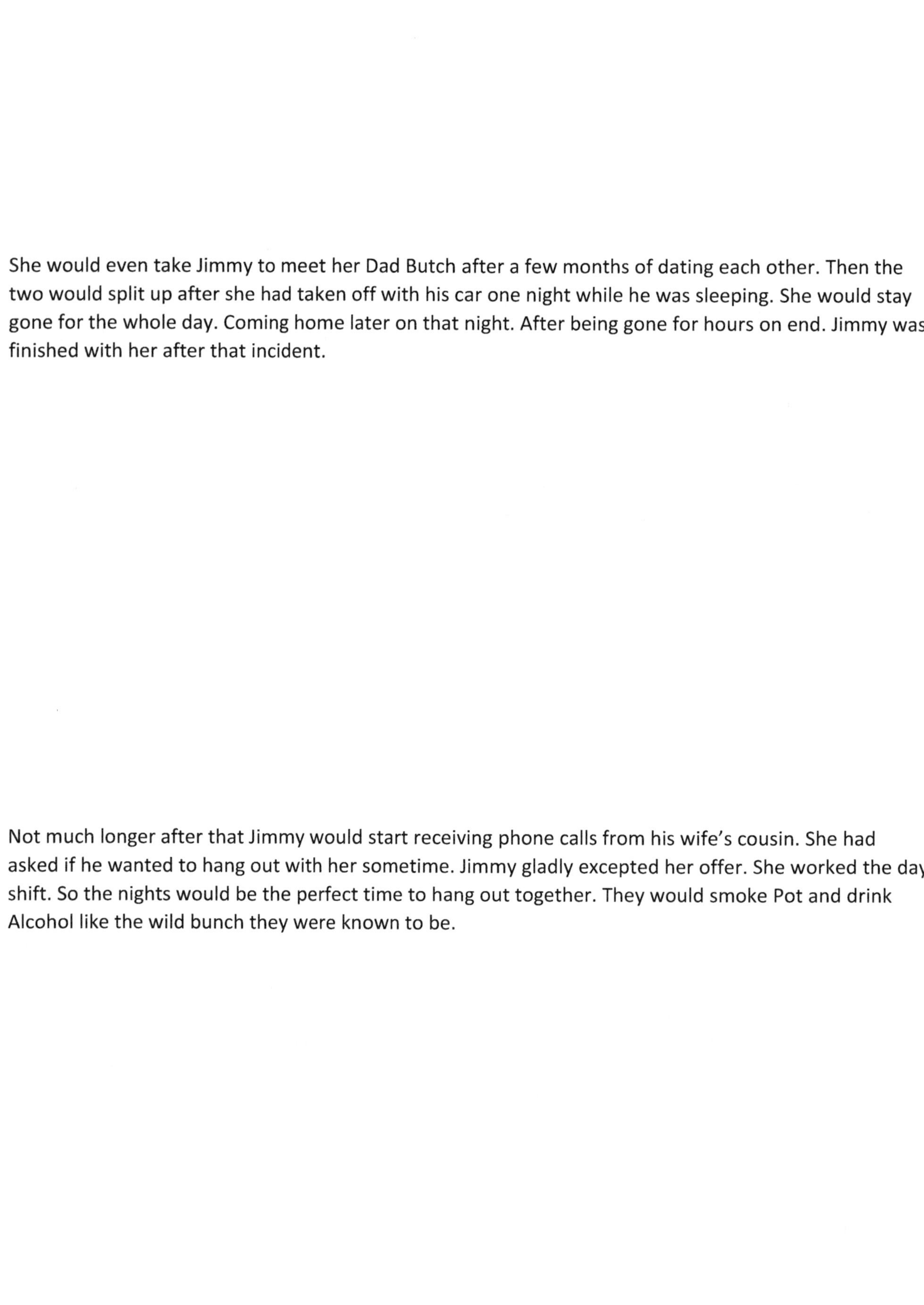

She would even take Jimmy to meet her Dad Butch after a few months of dating each other. Then the two would split up after she had taken off with his car one night while he was sleeping. She would stay gone for the whole day. Coming home later on that night. After being gone for hours on end. Jimmy was finished with her after that incident.

Not much longer after that Jimmy would start receiving phone calls from his wife's cousin. She had asked if he wanted to hang out with her sometime. Jimmy gladly excepted her offer. She worked the day shift. So the nights would be the perfect time to hang out together. They would smoke Pot and drink Alcohol like the wild bunch they were known to be.

One night while over at a party on the other side of town. They were together again Jimmy and Melanie. Partying like maniacs all of them together. Melanie had pulled Jimmy off to the side. As she now started to tell him how she had always wanted him in her bed. But that he had gone and married her cousin.

(Chapter 11)

Jimmy was flattered so much he even blushed in that moment. Soon after telling him what she had waited so long to do. Melanie had ended the party early. Making everyone leave quickly. She was clearly ready for something. At the time she was locking up the front door. Melanie's friend Lacey had taken Jimmy through the house as if she were giving him a tour.

As she showed him the bathroom she now started to kiss him. As she closed the door behind her. She quickly took off her shirt and bra and shorts as well. And grabbed Jimmy's hand. Shoving it down her panties. Guiding his hand to her vagina. She took his hand and rubbed it across her labia over and over again. Quicker with each movement.

As she started to moan the bathroom door opened in a flash. Their stood Melanie as she stared at the two of them. Immediately telling Jimmy to come on as she took his hand and led him into the bedroom. Pushing him on the bed as she now undressed. She turned out the lights and pulled him to her. She really wanted him in that moment.

Quickly she pulled the covers down as she pushed his head lower down her body. She wanted him to kiss her labia as she guided his lips to her hotness. And he did so with an instant passion. He had always liked her but, had never been given the chance until now. He would make the most of this night. Even if his soon to be ex wife found out he didn't care.

Jimmy had been so angry with how they had split up and the reason behind it. He made love to Melanie all night long. And in the morning Melanie said that she had no regrets at all. That her cousin was a bitch. For keeping his two Son's away from him. She told him he was a good father. And that his wife had been cheating for some time now.

(Chapter 12)

He was mad for a few moments after she had told him his wife was a cheater. But then he just decided that he would let it be known that he had an affair with her. A bit further down the road. After the two of them had courted for a month or two. He continued to see her for months. Jimmy would quite often find himself at Melanie's moms house. Spending the nights with her.

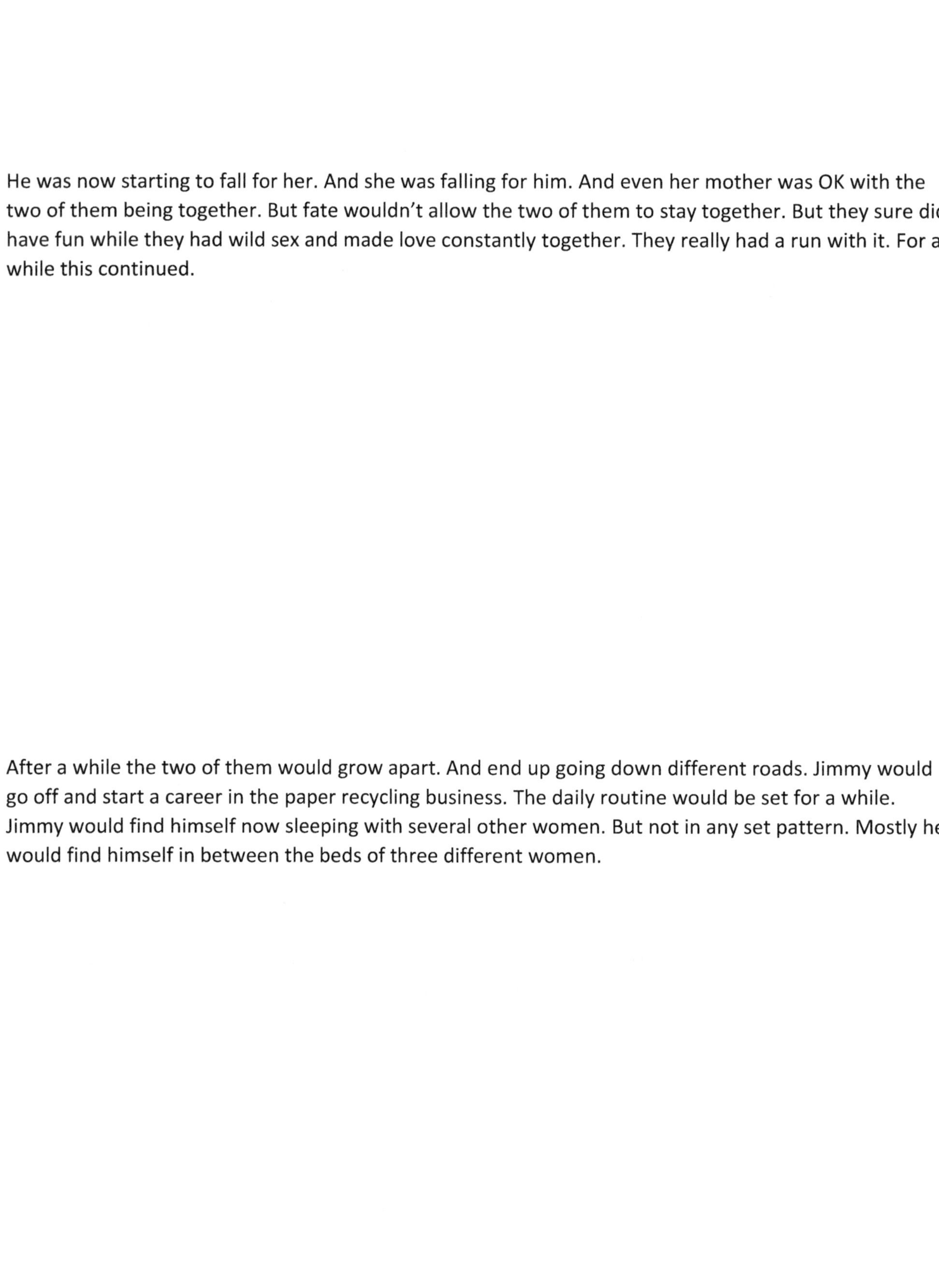

He was now starting to fall for her. And she was falling for him. And even her mother was OK with the two of them being together. But fate wouldn't allow the two of them to stay together. But they sure did have fun while they had wild sex and made love constantly together. They really had a run with it. For a while this continued.

After a while the two of them would grow apart. And end up going down different roads. Jimmy would go off and start a career in the paper recycling business. The daily routine would be set for a while. Jimmy would find himself now sleeping with several other women. But not in any set pattern. Mostly he would find himself in between the beds of three different women.

And then every once in a while another woman would come along his path. The weekdays would bring work and the weekends would bring play. Hitting the gravel pits. Or a local bowling alley in town. Having a blast and drinking heavily through the hours of the night. Usually bedding a woman along the weekend. Jimmy was a very wild young man.

Life would catch up to him. Child support would get on his ass and never cut him loose again. Sending him to jail very many times. And even a two year stint in prison would come along in due time. Life for him would be a total hell for a long time. Jimmy would almost have a nervous breakdown over the court system harassing him all of the damn time.

(Chapter 13)

He had spent so much damn time being incarcerated by the courts over such simple bullshit. Ohio, was such a shit State when it came to handling the laws of the country. They would give a murderer Fifteen years for Murder. And turn around an hour later and try to give a man 12 years for Non-Support of dependents.

It was sad no doubts about it. It was totally the truth. And even the people that tried the cases would even laugh about it. “Hell” his lawyer had said to him on one such occasion. “You would have been better off just Killing someone”. That was a totally true statement at that certain time. And Jimmy had agreed with his lawyer in that very moment. That he most definetly had a point.

They had in fact tried to give Jimmy Twelve years for not paying his child support. Back in the year of 2004. The deal they had been able to hammer out with the court was 3 years after fighting tooth and nail. In which he were sent up the river shortly thereafter. On up to Lancaster penitentiary in North Eastern Ohio. Jimmy would be lucky and get a program. A project named Camp Reams had taken him in.

It was a very grueling program to say the very least. It was setup as if it were just as basic training for members joining the military. Running and working out. And then more running followed by more working out yet again. Followed by school in the evening and then more working out again. This place tore one down and built them back up quickly.

And the program was setup in order to do so much in only a matter of no more than Ninety days tops. Then and only then if one did all that was asked of them then they would be released. School was another major factor in the program. The school program had to be passed if one wanted to leave at the Ninety day mark.

Jimmy would continue on and stop his battle with the court. They had came at him with a decent deal. And he had accepted it. He would make his way up the river to the Penitentiary. Do his program and be home in Eight months tops. He had to sit at the O.D.R.C. Ohio Department Of Rehabilitation And Corrections for a couple of months.

When they finally made room for him to go. He was bussed out on a Friday morning. And he would find himself at the bottom of the hill from Lancaster penitentiary in North Eastern Ohio later that day. As soon as the bunch that got off of the bus that had taken the group there. The Drill Instructors came running outside.

It was time to be worn down. Stripped of all pride. And then the process of rebuilding would soon start shortly after the fact. The whole group and Jimmy were told to get down. As the drill instructor now made them do push-ups until they puked or fell flat on their faces. Whichever came first. If you quit or gave up. You went up on the hill.

Lancaster prison would be the next destination. Where you would find yourself doing every day of your time. Jimmy never flinched that day. He had been working out the whole time while at C.R.C. He wasn't going to allow them to break him on that day. He had never been so focused on a task. He pushed forward in every single thing he was asked to do that morning.

He would be a ghost for seven days. And then if he made it. He would get his uniform and get out of the orange jumpsuit. Which was very uncomfortable in fact. Jimmy pushed through the Ninety day program. And come home on April 16th. The first night he was out was spent back in the county jail. Hamilton County Justice Center Sheriff's Office had traveled all of the way up there to grab him.

(Chapter 15)

They had in fact forgotten that they had placed him there. And so he would be picked up and taken down to Queensgate Jail until the next morning. He arrived at court and explained just exactly where he had been for almost a year. And the Judge set him free soon after the hearing was over and done with. Jimmy would go back over to Jail to grab his stuff.

And then taken back to the Justice Center to be let go. His first day out would be a trip. Before he could even hit the front door. A buddy had showed up to take him out to drink and Celebrate his first day out. Jimmy would find himself snorting an Oxy 40 MG. Right off of the back of the bar toilet. Just a few hours later.

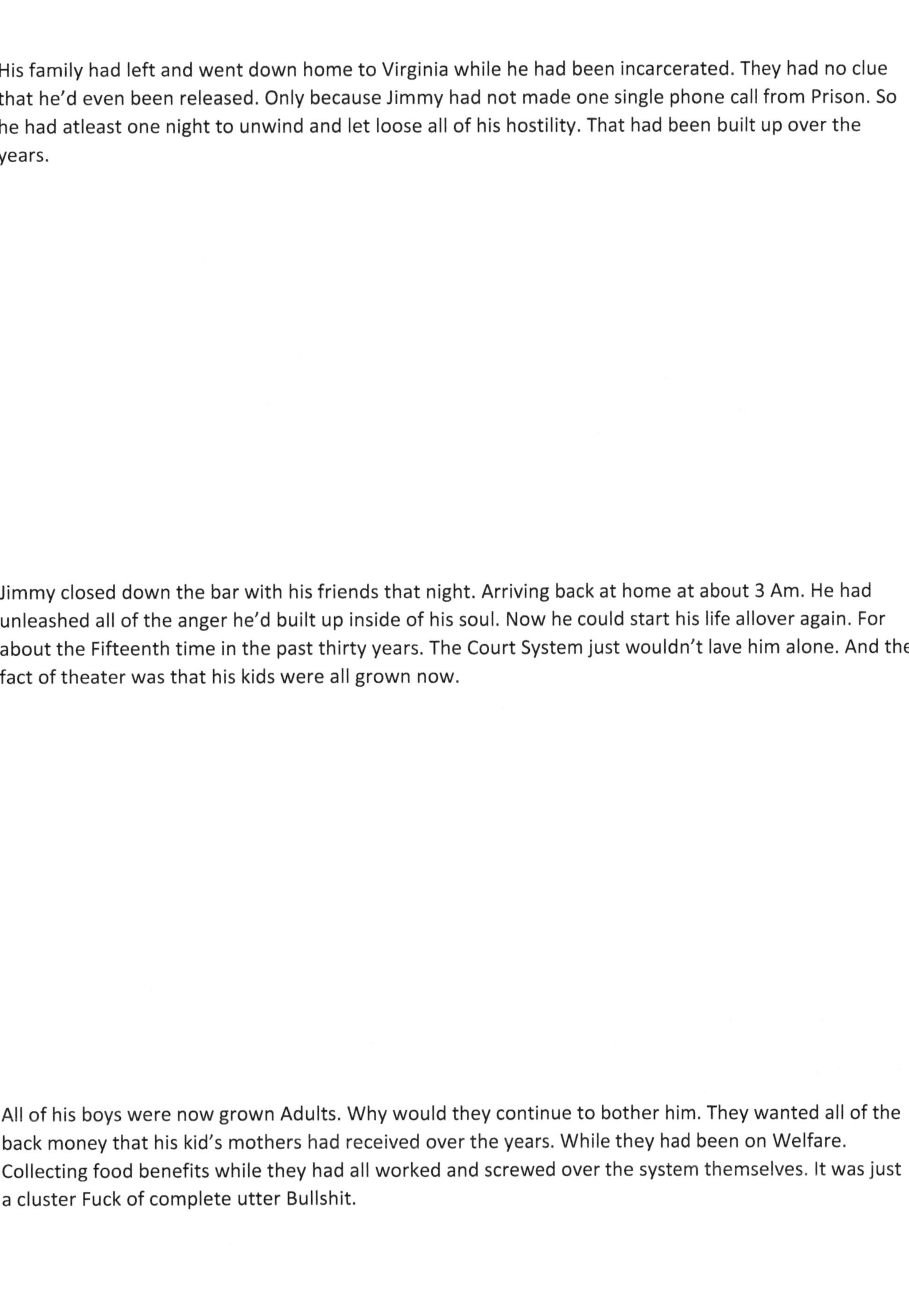

His family had left and went down home to Virginia while he had been incarcerated. They had no clue that he'd even been released. Only because Jimmy had not made one single phone call from Prison. So he had atleast one night to unwind and let loose all of his hostility. That had been built up over the years.

Jimmy closed down the bar with his friends that night. Arriving back at home at about 3 Am. He had unleashed all of the anger he'd built up inside of his soul. Now he could start his life allover again. For about the Fifteenth time in the past thirty years. The Court System just wouldn't lave him alone. And the fact of theater was that his kids were all grown now.

All of his boys were now grown Adults. Why would they continue to bother him. They wanted all of the back money that his kid's mothers had received over the years. While they had been on Welfare. Collecting food benefits while they had all worked and screwed over the system themselves. It was just a cluster Fuck of complete utter Bullshit.

Anything for pay back was how Jimmy had looked at it. For him leaving each of them. Not staying and being part of their lives. Jimmy was growing so sick and tired of going through this shit. They all had grown to despise him. He had left them all and became an Author. A writer of children's books. And adult books as well also.

(Chapter 16)

He had become a success almost overnight. His first Book ever would be sought out by very many of his friends. Then from there he just kept on pushing forward. And over the period of just under a year and a half. He would write and complete well over 55 books. Different Subjects and spread them out over many different age groups.

He then would be pulled in and messed with by the courts allover again. Which couldn't come at a worse time. Just when Jimmy had thought the worst was finally behind him. Once and for all. Here it came again, knocking the wind out of him for sure. Jimmy thought that it was all over finally. That the courts would maybe leave him alone.

They had shown him once again that their thirst for money was still strong. They were pulling him back in to court yet again. For Non payment of support. The issue Jimmy was having was that his kids were now men. Their was no reason for this shit so he had thought. This was the 3rd time in under a year that they had pulled him into court.

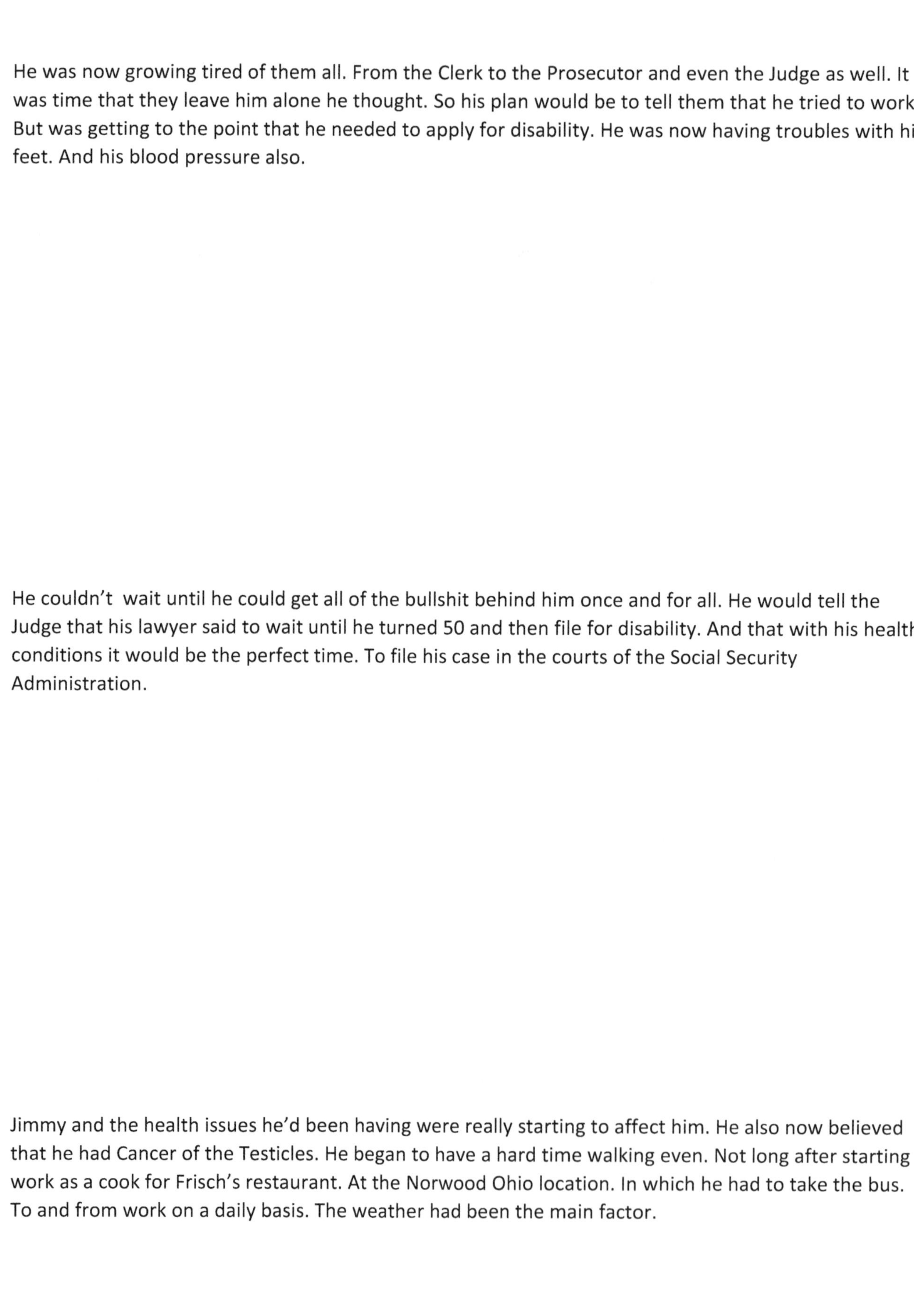

He was now growing tired of them all. From the Clerk to the Prosecutor and even the Judge as well. It was time that they leave him alone he thought. So his plan would be to tell them that he tried to work. But was getting to the point that he needed to apply for disability. He was now having troubles with his feet. And his blood pressure also.

He couldn't wait until he could get all of the bullshit behind him once and for all. He would tell the Judge that his lawyer said to wait until he turned 50 and then file for disability. And that with his health conditions it would be the perfect time. To file his case in the courts of the Social Security Administration.

Jimmy and the health issues he'd been having were really starting to affect him. He also now believed that he had Cancer of the Testicles. He began to have a hard time walking even. Not long after starting work as a cook for Frisch's restaurant. At the Norwood Ohio location. In which he had to take the bus. To and from work on a daily basis. The weather had been the main factor.

(Chapter 17)

Jimmy had a huge turn for the worst with his health issues. They had came on just after surgery to Fix a hernia. The Surgeon told Jimmy to get his prostate checked. But Jimmy pushed it off and had let it go. Now he was worried over his health. Several issues had risen over the past few months. And when his blood pressure had risen off and on over the past few months.

He decided to listen to his lawyer and go ahead with the choice to file for disability. Jimmy clearly couldn't make a go of work any longer. He had to file now if he wanted any chance to get his case on file. While he was going through the other court issues at the time. He wanted everything to be in the process of getting to the finish line.

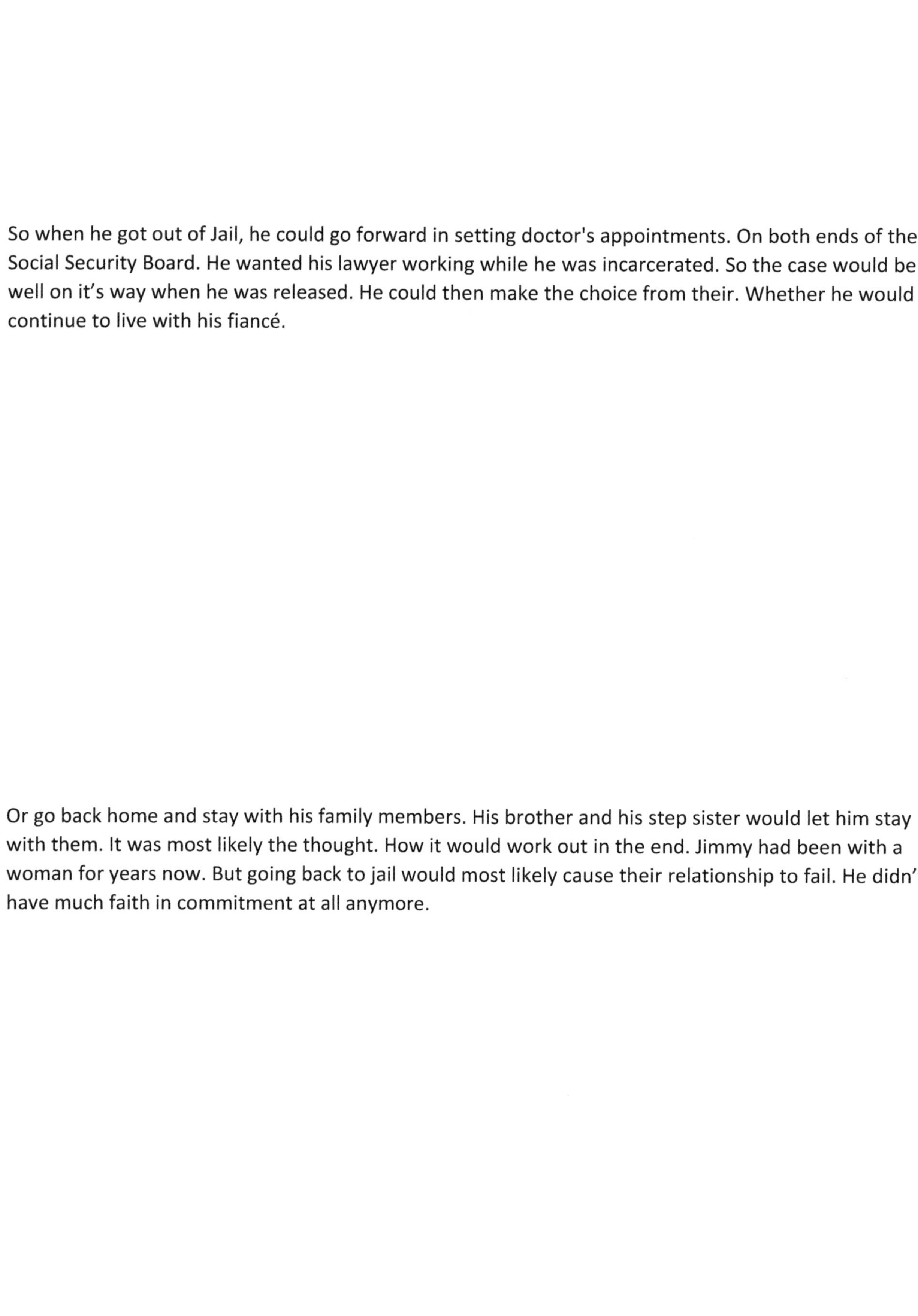

So when he got out of Jail, he could go forward in setting doctor's appointments. On both ends of the Social Security Board. He wanted his lawyer working while he was incarcerated. So the case would be well on it's way when he was released. He could then make the choice from their. Whether he would continue to live with his fiancé.

Or go back home and stay with his family members. His brother and his step sister would let him stay with them. It was most likely the thought. How it would work out in the end. Jimmy had been with a woman for years now. But going back to jail would most likely cause their relationship to fail. He didn't have much faith in commitment at all anymore.

After all it had went exactly like that once before. He had went to Jail. And after about a week of being locked up. His Fiancé had taken off and went out on a date with another man. So Jimmy figure it would be the same road taken once again this time. Their was just no luck in his life at this time. Other than the fact that. He did now have several Books available in most of the local stores at this time.

And didn't even have an open bank account to collect his money from his Book sales. Everyone felt like something or someone was holding him back. The feeling was that of envy in all honesty. Jimmy now had a lot of friends who had now become so called haters. Which to his face they would act happy for him. But behind his back they talked shit about him.

(Chapter 18)

Jimmy had just started several projects. And had finished several others as well. Writings that had become works of progress. He had several books that had been recently moved over to Barnes and Noble Book stores for sale. And other Books also. The work he had completed had just gained a little bit of popularity as of late. That is exactly what Jimmy had wanted to happen.

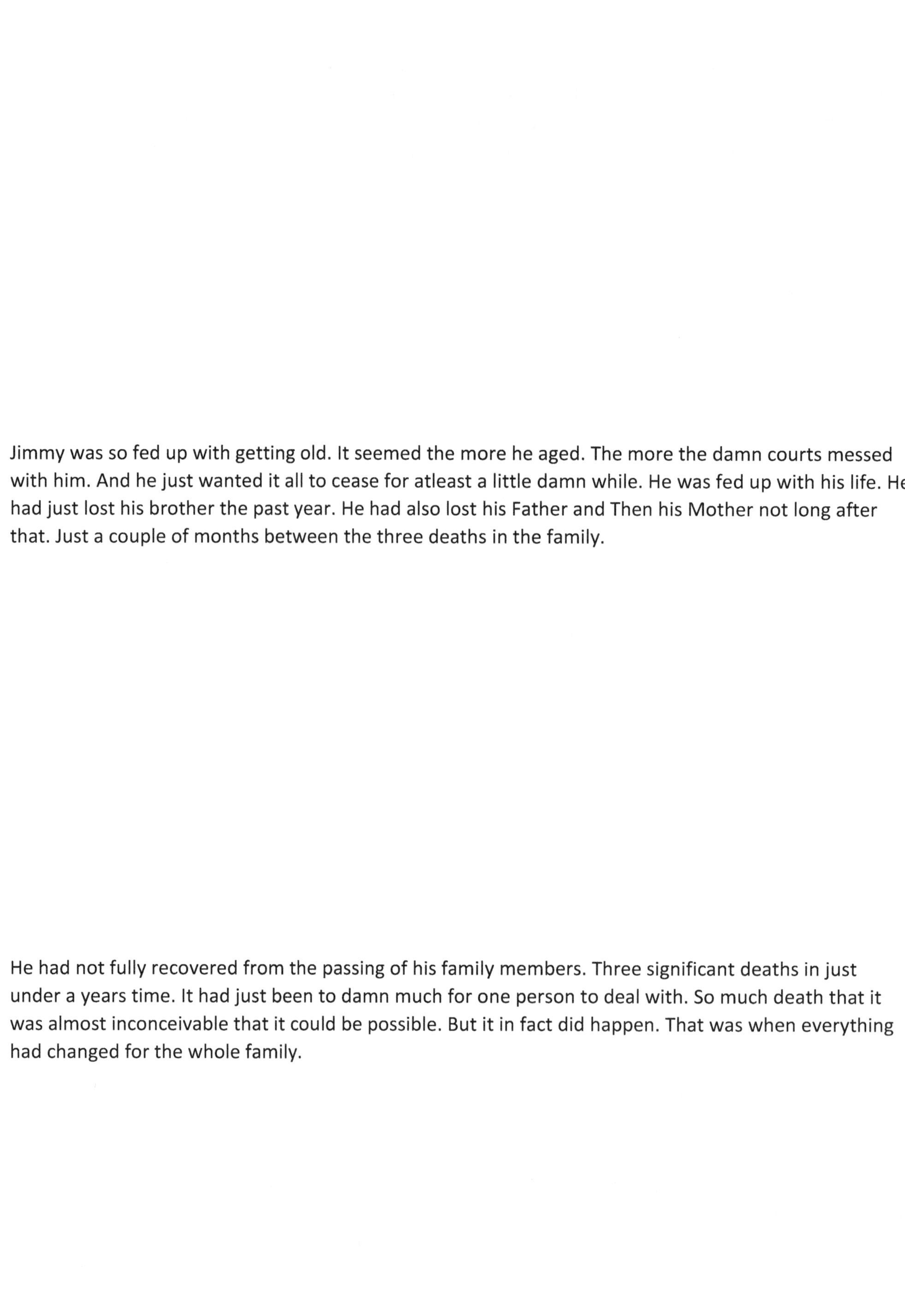

Jimmy was so fed up with getting old. It seemed the more he aged. The more the damn courts messed with him. And he just wanted it all to cease for atleast a little damn while. He was fed up with his life. He had just lost his brother the past year. He had also lost his Father and Then his Mother not long after that. Just a couple of months between the three deaths in the family.

He had not fully recovered from the passing of his family members. Three significant deaths in just under a years time. It had just been to damn much for one person to deal with. So much death that it was almost inconceivable that it could be possible. But it in fact did happen. That was when everything had changed for the whole family.

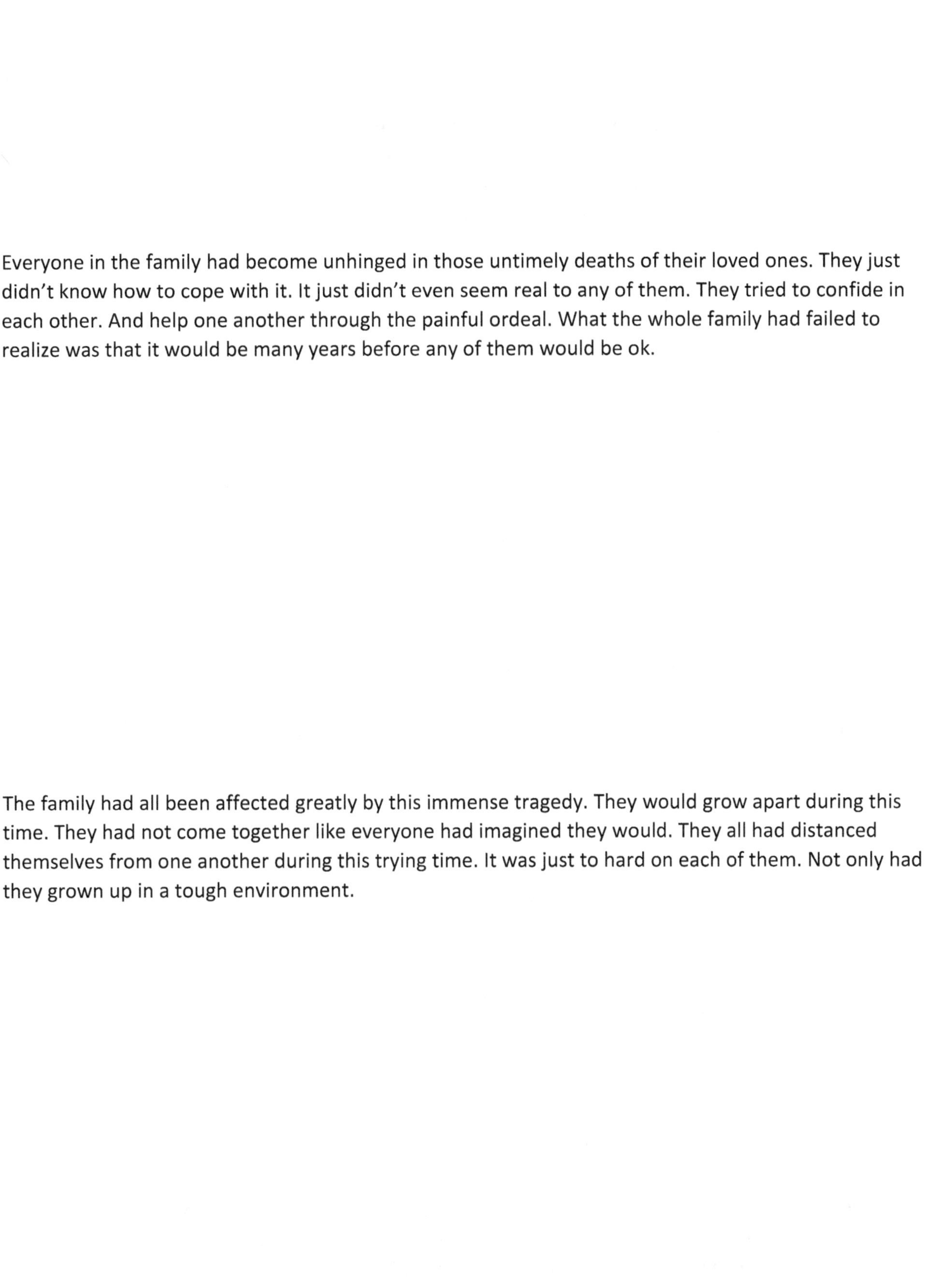

Everyone in the family had become unhinged in those untimely deaths of their loved ones. They just didn't know how to cope with it. It just didn't even seem real to any of them. They tried to confide in each other. And help one another through the painful ordeal. What the whole family had failed to realize was that it would be many years before any of them would be ok.

The family had all been affected greatly by this immense tragedy. They would grow apart during this time. They had not come together like everyone had imagined they would. They all had distanced themselves from one another during this trying time. It was just to hard on each of them. Not only had they grown up in a tough environment.

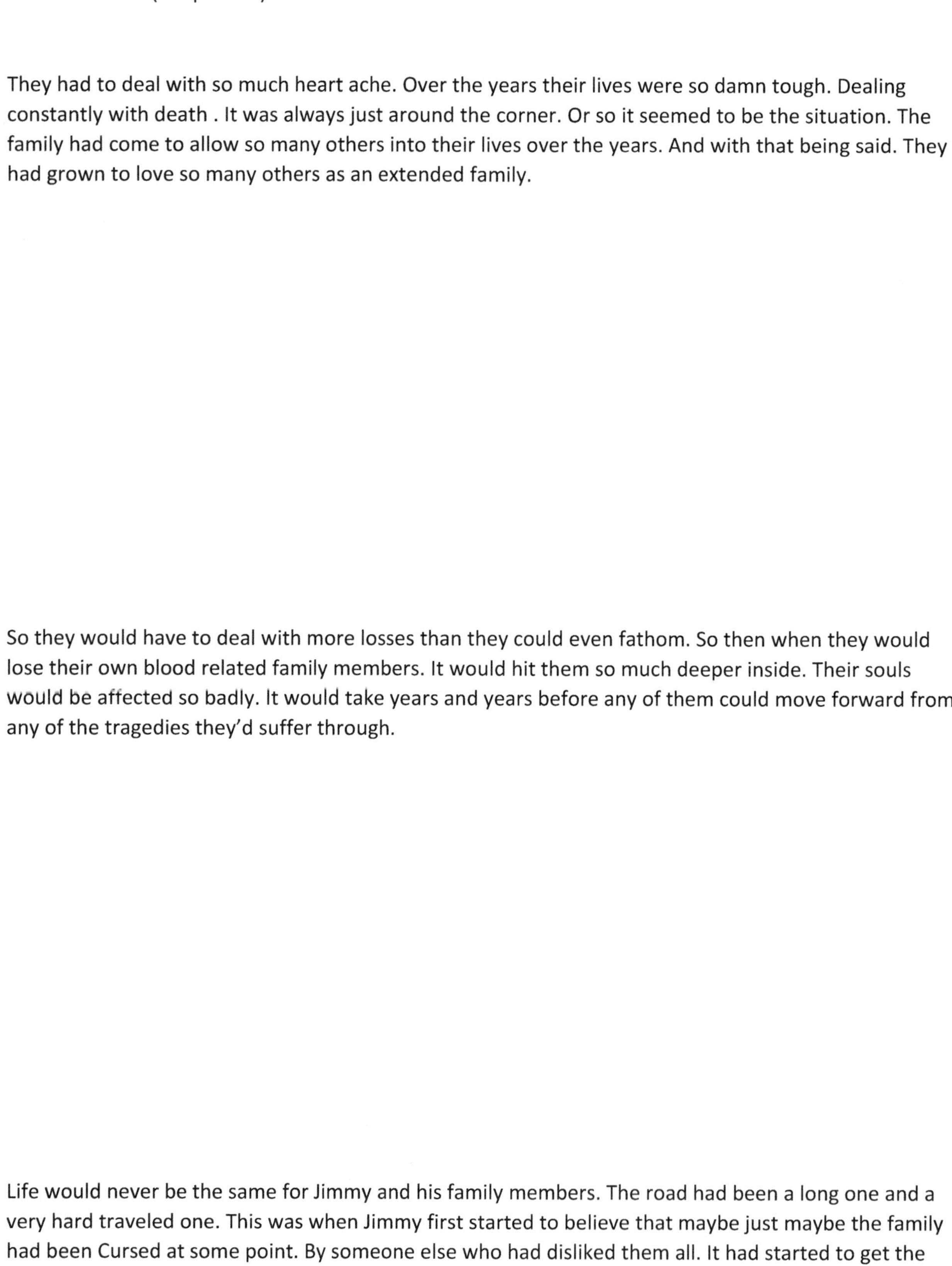

(Chapter 19)

They had to deal with so much heart ache. Over the years their lives were so damn tough. Dealing constantly with death . It was always just around the corner. Or so it seemed to be the situation. The family had come to allow so many others into their lives over the years. And with that being said. They had grown to love so many others as an extended family.

So they would have to deal with more losses than they could even fathom. So then when they would lose their own blood related family members. It would hit them so much deeper inside. Their souls would be affected so badly. It would take years and years before any of them could move forward from any of the tragedies they'd suffer through.

Life would never be the same for Jimmy and his family members. The road had been a long one and a very hard traveled one. This was when Jimmy first started to believe that maybe just maybe the family had been Cursed at some point. By someone else who had disliked them all. It had started to get the entire family thinking of the possibility.

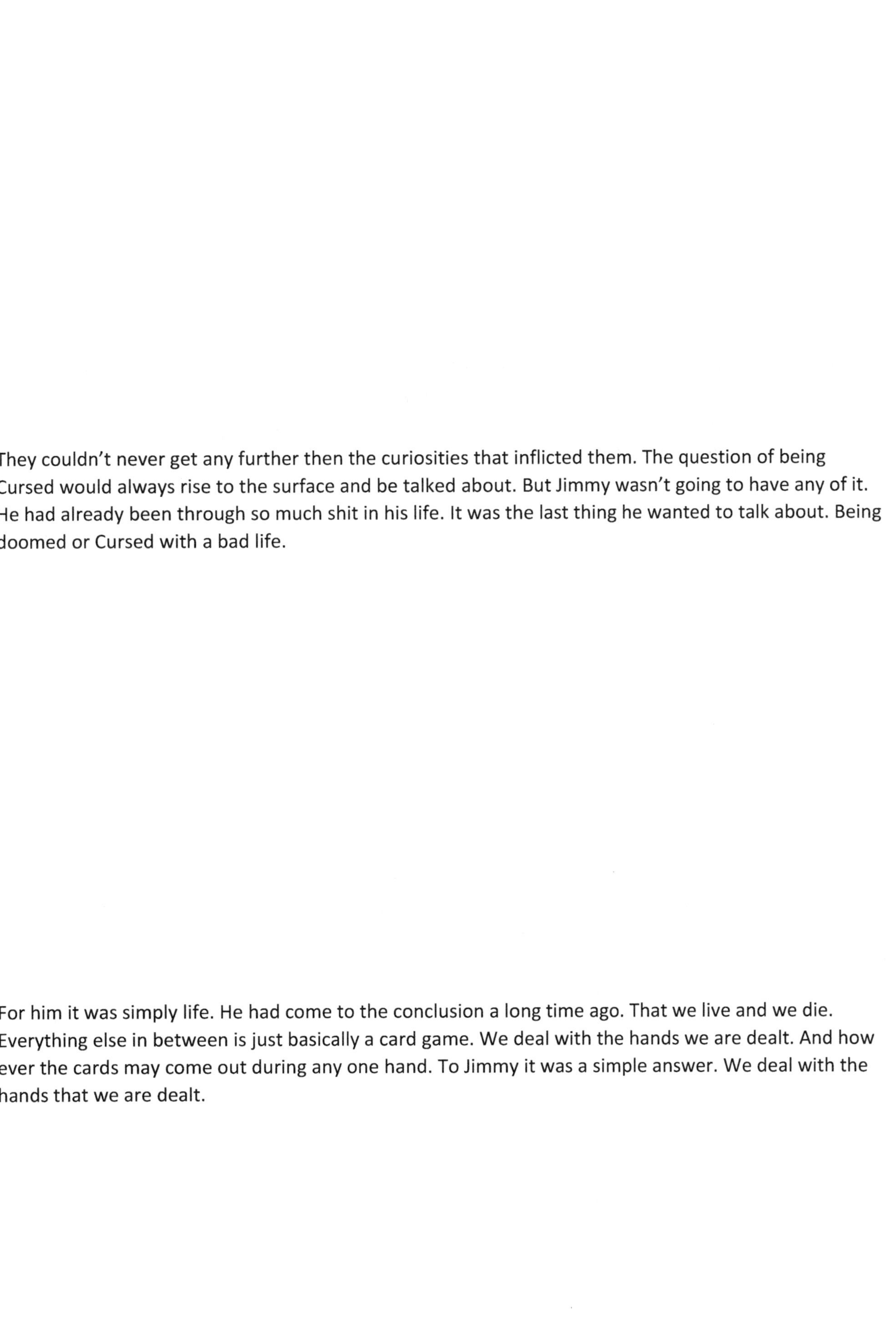

They couldn't never get any further then the curiosities that inflicted them. The question of being Cursed would always rise to the surface and be talked about. But Jimmy wasn't going to have any of it. He had already been through so much shit in his life. It was the last thing he wanted to talk about. Being doomed or Cursed with a bad life.

For him it was simply life. He had come to the conclusion a long time ago. That we live and we die. Everything else in between is just basically a card game. We deal with the hands we are dealt. And how ever the cards may come out during any one hand. To Jimmy it was a simple answer. We deal with the hands that we are dealt.

(Chapter 20)

To him that was all he could do about that. Life had always been hard. Not much of anything good ever came his families way. Hand me down cloths and a shitty twenty dollar Christmas for each kid while growing up under the same roof together. Watching the other kids at Grandma's house while each of the other kids got a 500.00 Christmas.

While my brothers and I received socks and flannel shirts to keep warm with. And at the end of the party. Some left over food to take home for the next few days. Just in case the kids had nothing to eat. They would make sure that the children had a little something in our belly. It wouldn't last forever. As Jimmie's Grandpa would pass away.

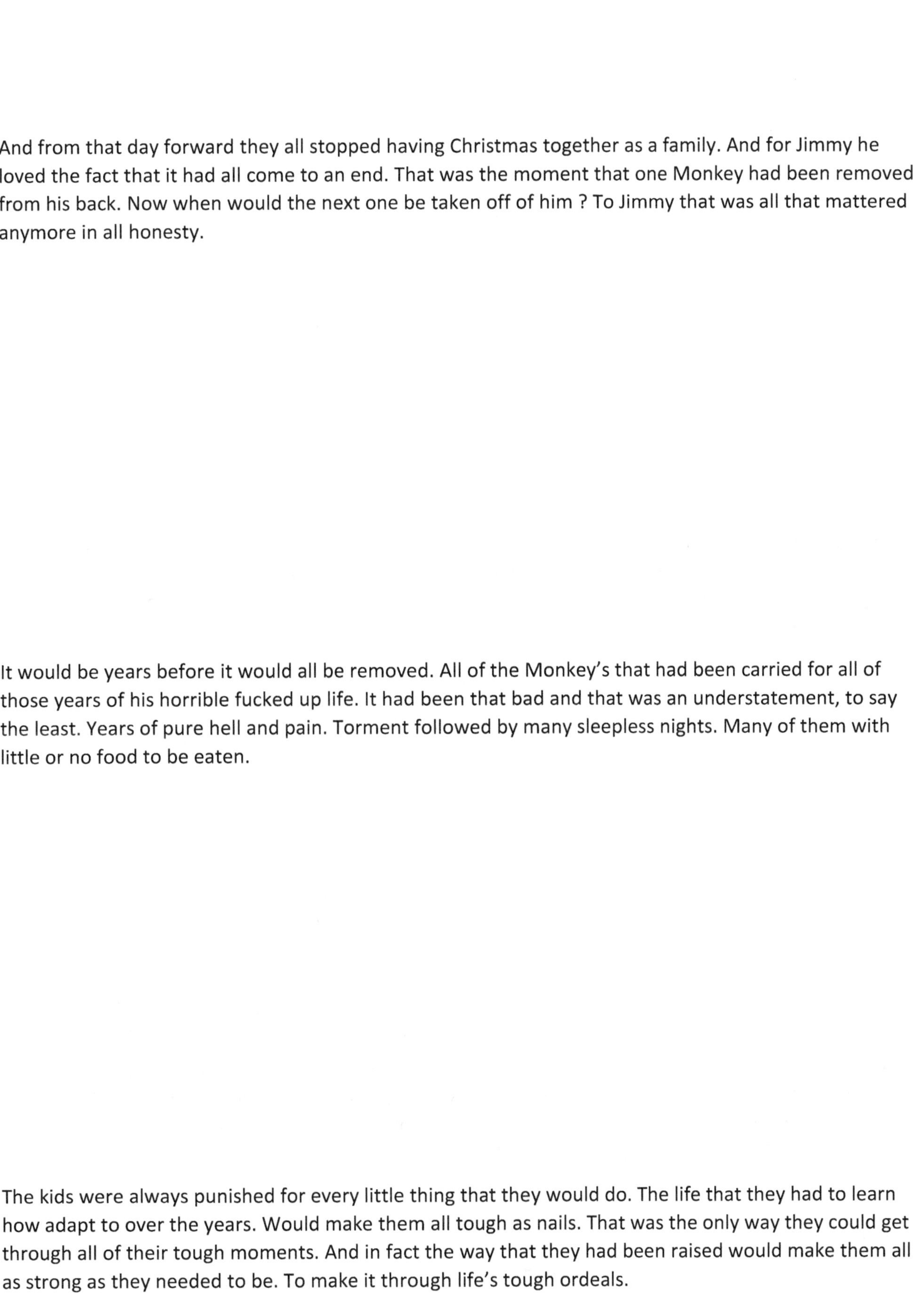

And from that day forward they all stopped having Christmas together as a family. And for Jimmy he loved the fact that it had all come to an end. That was the moment that one Monkey had been removed from his back. Now when would the next one be taken off of him ? To Jimmy that was all that mattered anymore in all honesty.

It would be years before it would all be removed. All of the Monkey's that had been carried for all of those years of his horrible fucked up life. It had been that bad and that was an understatement, to say the least. Years of pure hell and pain. Torment followed by many sleepless nights. Many of them with little or no food to be eaten.

The kids were always punished for every little thing that they would do. The life that they had to learn how adapt to over the years. Would make them all tough as nails. That was the only way they could get through all of their tough moments. And in fact the way that they had been raised would make them all as strong as they needed to be. To make it through life's tough ordeals.

(Chapter 21)

None of the kids had a clue. That their lives would become a rude ass awakening at a certain point. Having kids of their own and having to worry about their safety day in and day out. Jimmy would end up having not 1 or 2 boys. But 5 of them with 4 different women. And in the very end. Jimmy would end up with the last woman he would have a child with.

And for the first years of the boy's life. Jimmy wouldn't even know if the child was his. That had been the sad part about it all. It would be well into the boys Teenage years before he would find out his last son was actually his for certain. From that day forward his life had started to change for once. Even through living with one of the most promiscuous girls in his hometown.

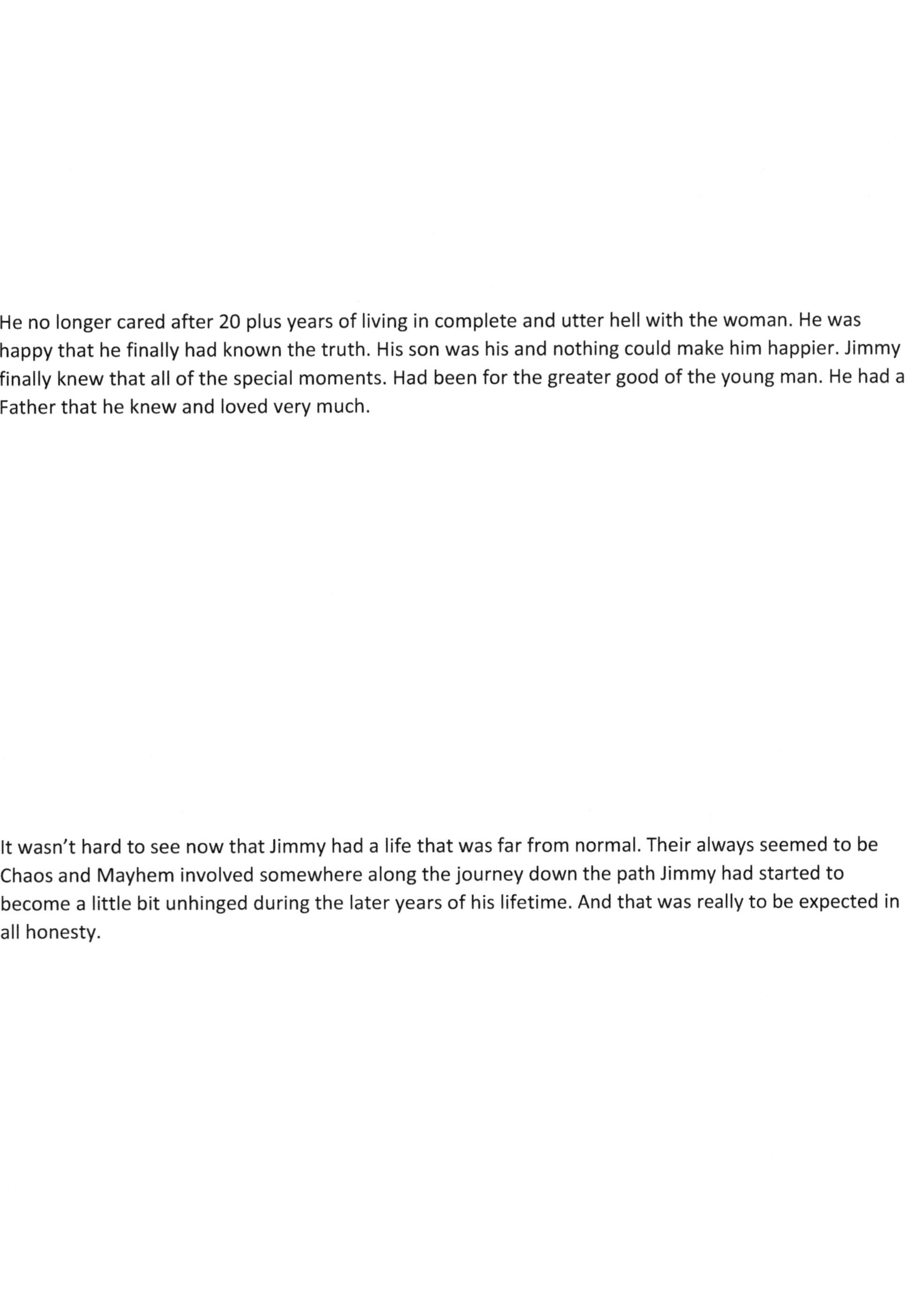

He no longer cared after 20 plus years of living in complete and utter hell with the woman. He was happy that he finally had known the truth. His son was his and nothing could make him happier. Jimmy finally knew that all of the special moments. Had been for the greater good of the young man. He had a Father that he knew and loved very much.

It wasn't hard to see now that Jimmy had a life that was far from normal. Their always seemed to be Chaos and Mayhem involved somewhere along the journey down the path Jimmy had started to become a little bit unhinged during the later years of his lifetime. And that was really to be expected in all honesty.

The old man now at 50 years of age. Had been put through some really horrible shit during his life. So many trials and tribulations during his youth. To much to really ever fully overcome. What would come of Jimmy at the ripe age of 50 and on further down the winding road of his later journey. Would their be more death and destruction ? Or would it finally settle down ?

(Chapter 22)

Jimmy knew better than that for sure no doubts about it. Death would never stop in life. For in life came death. And he knew that. But hated the fact that he had experienced way to many deaths in his 50 years on Earth. Honestly it had been to many to count. And that was mainly what had bothered him so badly along the way.

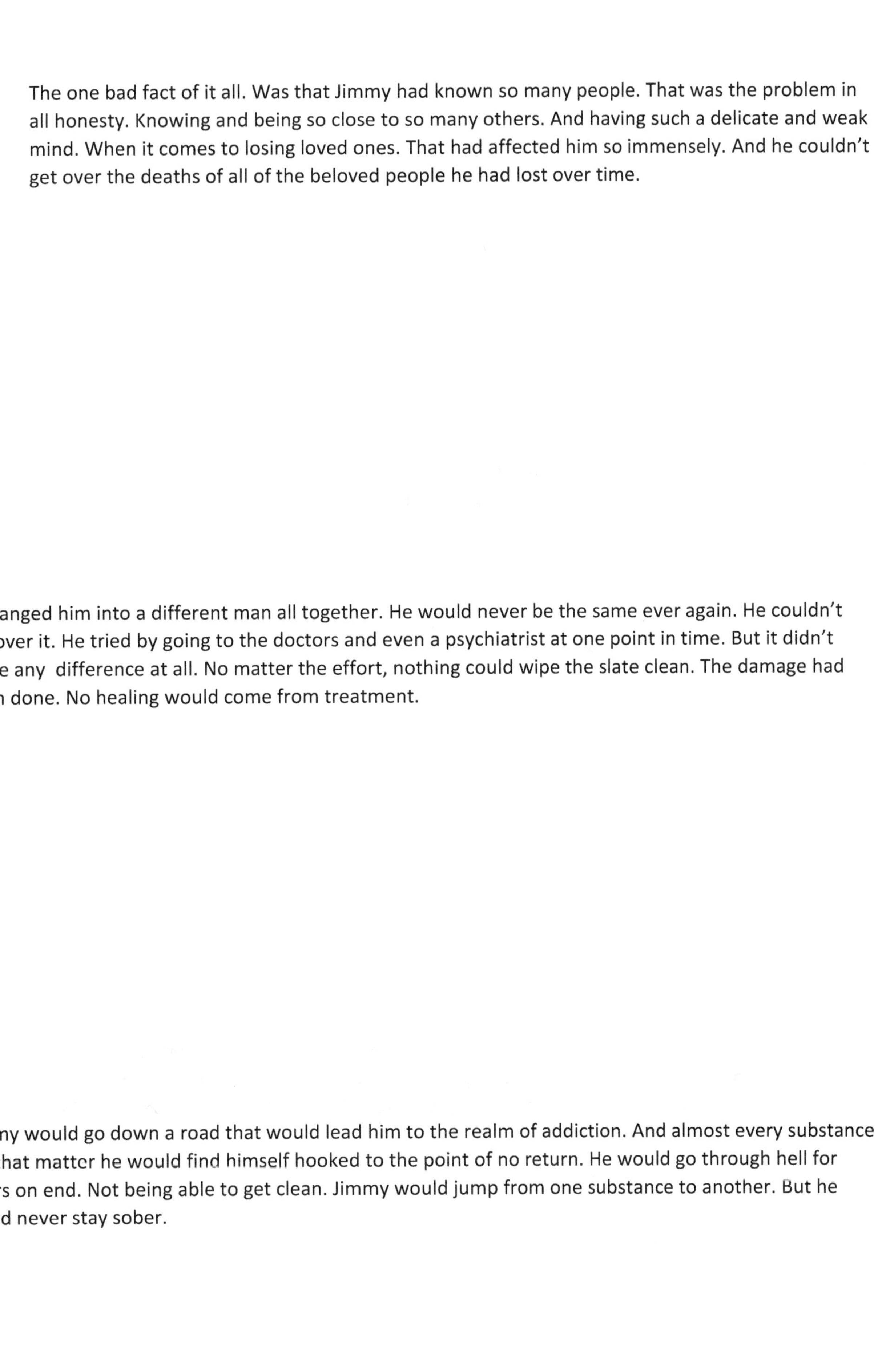

The one bad fact of it all. Was that Jimmy had known so many people. That was the problem in all honesty. Knowing and being so close to so many others. And having such a delicate and weak mind. When it comes to losing loved ones. That had affected him so immensely. And he couldn't get over the deaths of all of the beloved people he had lost over time.

It changed him into a different man all together. He would never be the same ever again. He couldn't get over it. He tried by going to the doctors and even a psychiatrist at one point in time. But it didn't make any difference at all. No matter the effort, nothing could wipe the slate clean. The damage had been done. No healing would come from treatment.

Jimmy would go down a road that would lead him to the realm of addiction. And almost every substance for that matter he would find himself hooked to the point of no return. He would go through hell for years on end. Not being able to get clean. Jimmy would jump from one substance to another. But he could never stay sober.

The battle would continue for over 12 years in total. It would be on one cold and Snowy Christmas Day. That Jimmy would wake up and say. I'm taking my life back today. From this moment forward. And not to long after that. Their would be another Monkey removed from his back. And in that moment Jimmy would feel so much better.

(Chapter 23)

In doing so Jimmy would put down all drugs. And he would also soon find his relationship with God once again. And as soon as he had found the Lord again. Their had been another Monkey thrown off of his back. Jimmy would start to rebuild his life again soon after. Things would finally start to get better soon after that all had taken place.

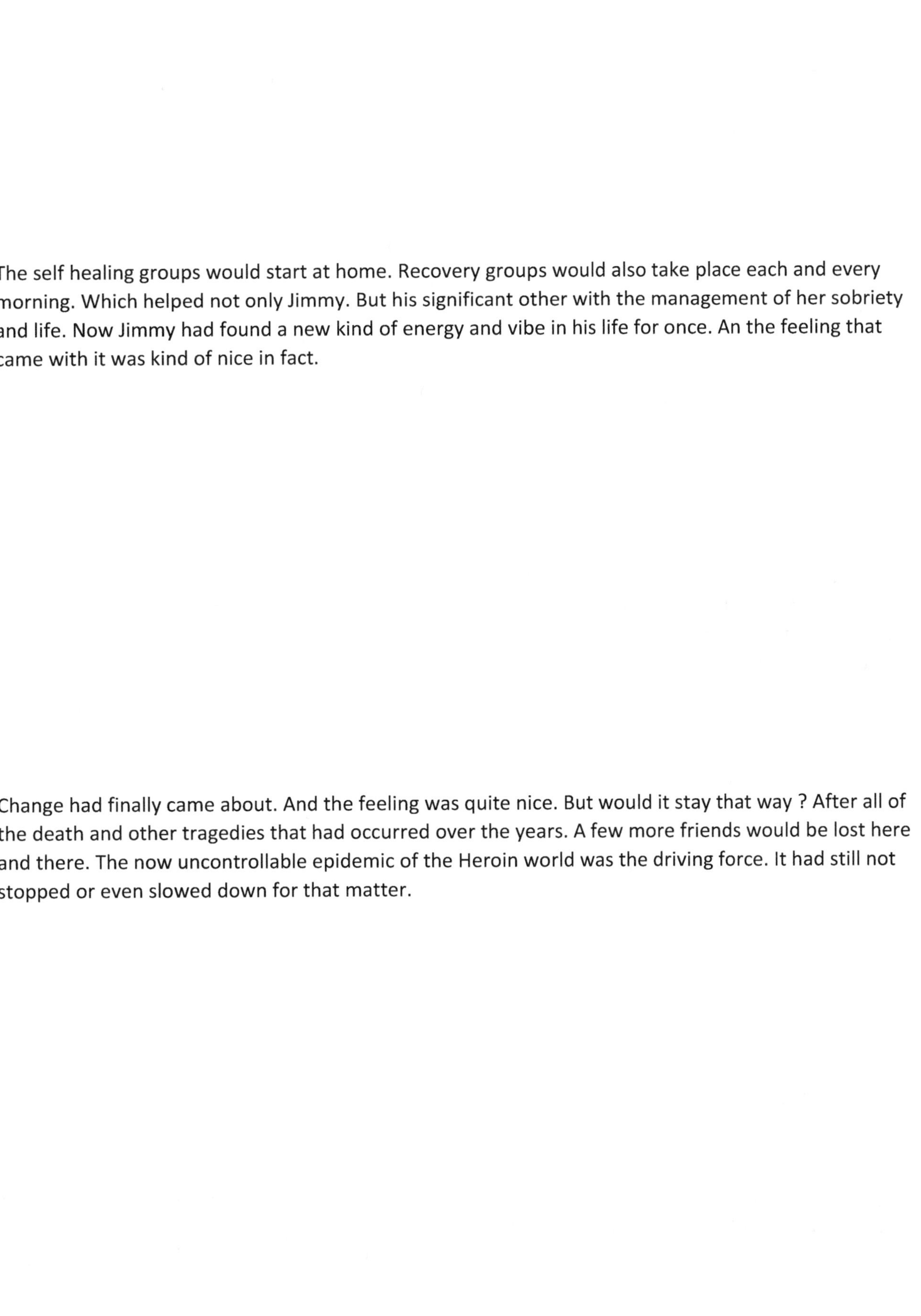

The self healing groups would start at home. Recovery groups would also take place each and every morning. Which helped not only Jimmy. But his significant other with the management of her sobriety and life. Now Jimmy had found a new kind of energy and vibe in his life for once. An the feeling that came with it was kind of nice in fact.

Change had finally came about. And the feeling was quite nice. But would it stay that way ? After all of the death and other tragedies that had occurred over the years. A few more friends would be lost here and there. The now uncontrollable epidemic of the Heroin world was the driving force. It had still not stopped or even slowed down for that matter.

So many friends and loved ones as well had died from the drug epidemic. Way to many for one person to handle. Jimmy had been close with so many people in his hometown. In fact Jimmy had watched so many of his friends die and had felt as if they were Cursed also. Their lives were very much a struggle. Day in and day out it seemed they all battled their Demon's.

They had all started to wonder if it was the town that they all lived in. That had been the reason for all of the bad luck. After all it had not been one or two years of bad luck. But their whole lives had been one disaster after another. The while group of friends and their loved ones also had gone through a lifetime of hell and torment. One after the other.

(Chapter 24)

Jimmy had known that all of his friends had lived a wild life style. Some of them had been stabbed. Some of them had been shot. Jimmy himself had been stabbed a total of 7 times. And had lived to tell his stories to others. The town they had all grew up in was known as Indian Territory back in the day. The Hopewell Indian tribe had called it home.

So that was the reason they had all suspected to be Cursed. Just by living there, on top of old Indian burial grounds. On the very top of the town sat a few Indian Mounds. They were named Long ago Indian Serpent Mounds. Their shapes consisting of that of a Snake. Would be the reason for the naming of them. It had been known that dead Indians were buried inside of those Mounds.

Along with other artifacts from the tribe. To be found by others who had came along later in the years. In the end of it all. That was now the belief now of the entire group of friends. That they had all been Cursed. Just for living in the area they had all grown up in. After all Jimmy had seen many friends leave the city. And over the years they'd been gone.

They had all ended up being successful in their lives. They had acquired homes for themselves and their children. And for the most part had thrived. But then one starts to miss their home town. And when being home sick makes one move back home. Soon after the move was made. The once upon a time successful person.

Had now become unhinged and found themselves in what seemed to be a never ending cycle of bad luck. They would now realize that their choice to move back home. Had been without a doubt. The worst choice they had ever made in their lifetime. But now also found themselves stuck in a horrible cycle. That couldn't be changed. They would have to ride out the storm.

(Chapter 25)

But the storm never seemed to end. That was the wild thing about the whole situation. The town for the most part experienced mostly bad luck. Not much good luck ever came to anyone in town. And even when it did bad luck would soon follow. As if a price had to be paid. For the little bit of good luck that had come along.

Their just always seemed to be a Monkey on Jimmy's back. And his friends backs as well. Back when they were all growing up as kids. Life was so much easier for them all. Even despite the Alcoholic fathers that most of them had. The friends of the group for the most part all had Alcoholic fathers. And that had seemed to be the reason for the kids all becoming friends so early in life.

They all would hang out with one another. The whole group lived so close together. In the same neighborhood. So they were always close together. So the hop skip and a jump made it easy for each of the friends to be there for one another. When any one of them had problems at home. Which with Alcoholic Fathers it would be quite often they would run to each others houses.

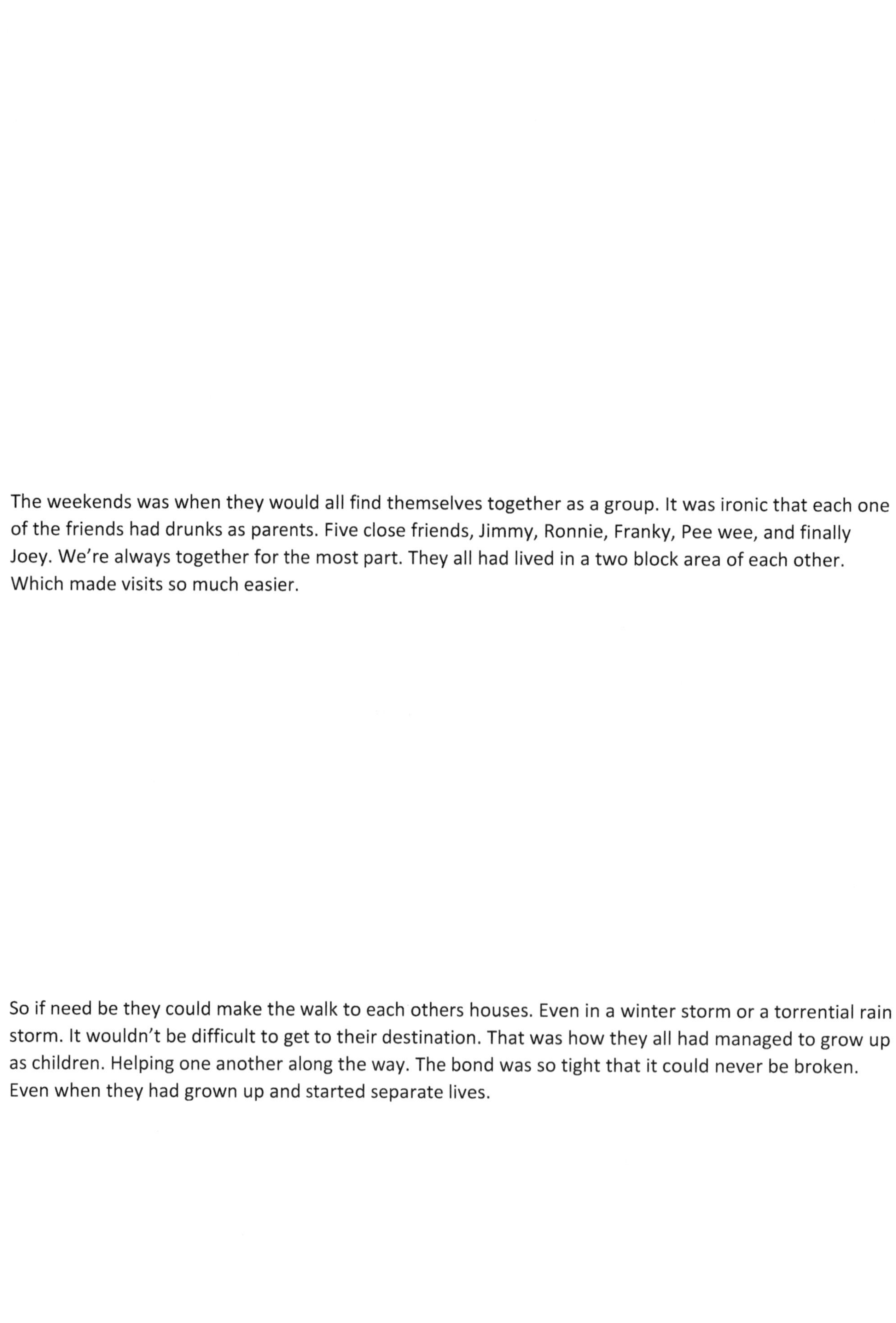

The weekends was when they would all find themselves together as a group. It was ironic that each one of the friends had drunks as parents. Five close friends, Jimmy, Ronnie, Franky, Pee wee, and finally Joey. We're always together for the most part. They all had lived in a two block area of each other. Which made visits so much easier.

So if need be they could make the walk to each others houses. Even in a winter storm or a torrential rain storm. It wouldn't be difficult to get to their destination. That was how they all had managed to grow up as children. Helping one another along the way. The bond was so tight that it could never be broken. Even when they had grown up and started separate lives.

Chapter 26)

With the new Internet systems up and running. They could all still be their for each other. And with only the click of a button was all that was needed. For Jimmy he now found himself facing another dilemma with the Court system once again. He had missed a Court appearance by way of a Zoom video meeting. His phone had shattered; Therefore he had no way to attend the meeting.

And soon after would have a Warrant issued for his arrest a few days after. Jimmy was once again caught in a catch 22. He had so much going on with his new health issues he was now dealing with. New blood pressure problems as well as now having foot issues. They were now feelings of his feet feeling raw when he would sit in his lounge chair.

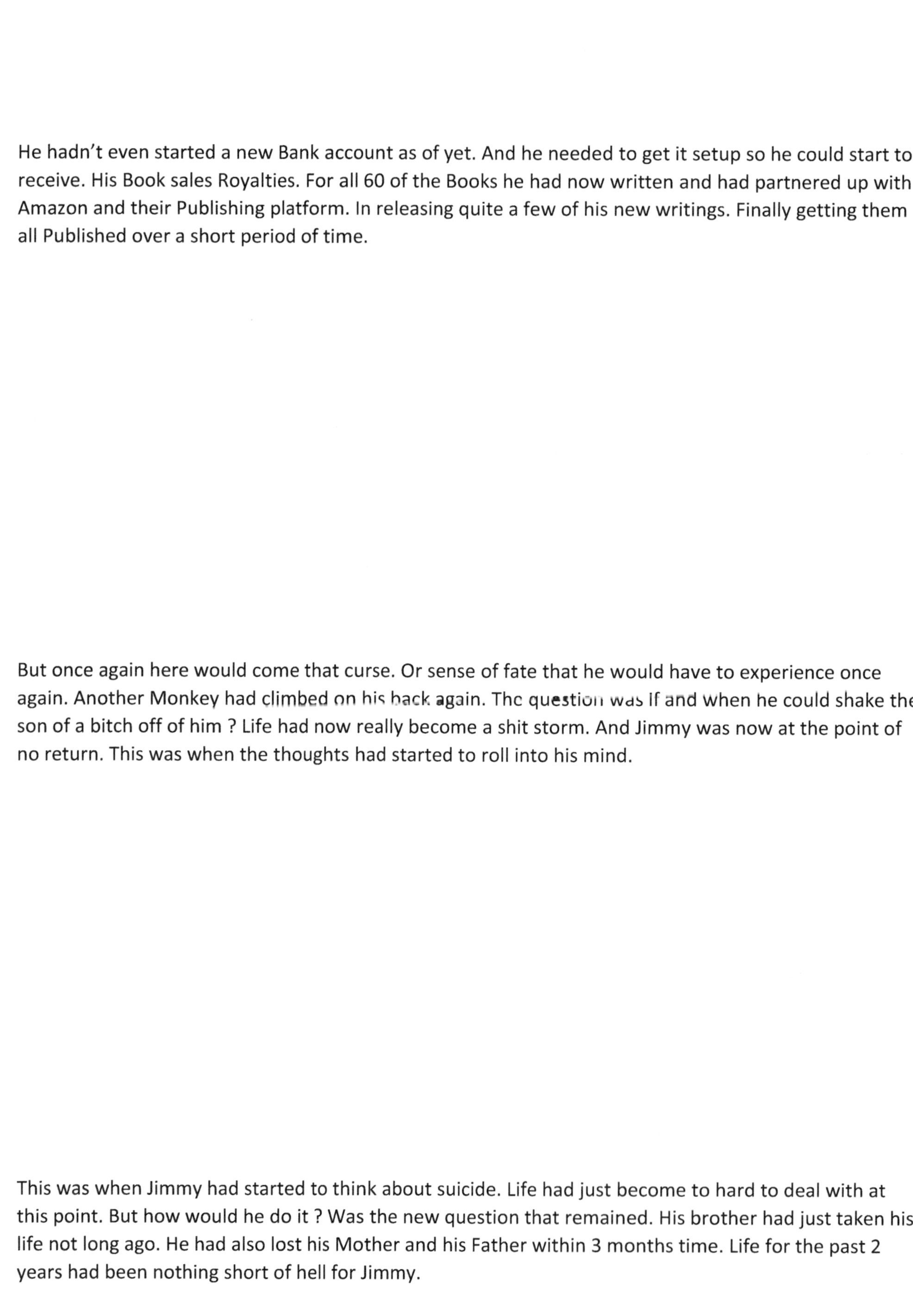

He hadn't even started a new Bank account as of yet. And he needed to get it setup so he could start to receive. His Book sales Royalties. For all 60 of the Books he had now written and had partnered up with Amazon and their Publishing platform. In releasing quite a few of his new writings. Finally getting them all Published over a short period of time.

But once again here would come that curse. Or sense of fate that he would have to experience once again. Another Monkey had climbed on his back again. The question was if and when he could shake the son of a bitch off of him ? Life had now really become a shit storm. And Jimmy was now at the point of no return. This was when the thoughts had started to roll into his mind.

This was when Jimmy had started to think about suicide. Life had just become to hard to deal with at this point. But how would he do it ? Was the new question that remained. His brother had just taken his life not long ago. He had also lost his Mother and his Father within 3 months time. Life for the past 2 years had been nothing short of hell for Jimmy.

(Chapter 27)

It had been in all honesty bitter sweet for the most part. A battle of survival had started shortly after the loss of his family members. Jimmy had become so lost not soon after burying them all together at a local cemetery site. It all had started to affect him when they made the drive from down off of the field that day. After the funeral, Jimmy watching his mothers casket sit at the top of the hill.

Slowly as it became smaller as they drove further and further away. As each second would slowly pass by. Until he could no longer see her casket. It had hit him like a ton of bricks right there in that moment. Sitting in a car, at the gates of the entrance to the cemetery. He was now feeling the exact impact of all 3 losses. Leaving him with a feeling of total helplessness.

Jimmy came back to reality; out of his daydream. He would then sit there for a few moments. Deciding what he would do next. The decision he would make, could mean life or death. If he did in fact choose to take his own life. He just couldn't imagine going back to Jail once again. This time it would be for just over 115 days.

Back to the same hell hole that he had just left a couple of years back. That was one thing he was unsure of. If at the age of just over 50 years old. If he could make it that many days without snapping. He had done everything he could trying to prepare himself. For one last trip back inside of the hell hole. He had even watched a few Locked up shows.

While trying to get ready for this next bit of time inside. He was unsure of how things would be upon his release. That had Jimmy really debating at the time. Of just what exactly to do with his life. Just another case of having that damn Monkey on his back again. It had been that situation his whole damn life. And that was the one thing he had grown so sick and tired of.

(Chapter 28)

He could never have a complete moment during his life. Where it didn't feel like a Monkey one was on him. Weighing him down in any way shape or form. Out of 50 damn years not a moment ever did he have any peace at all. If so, only a few slim moments If ever any was his thought about it. He was now stuck in the moment about to make one of the hardest decisions of his life.

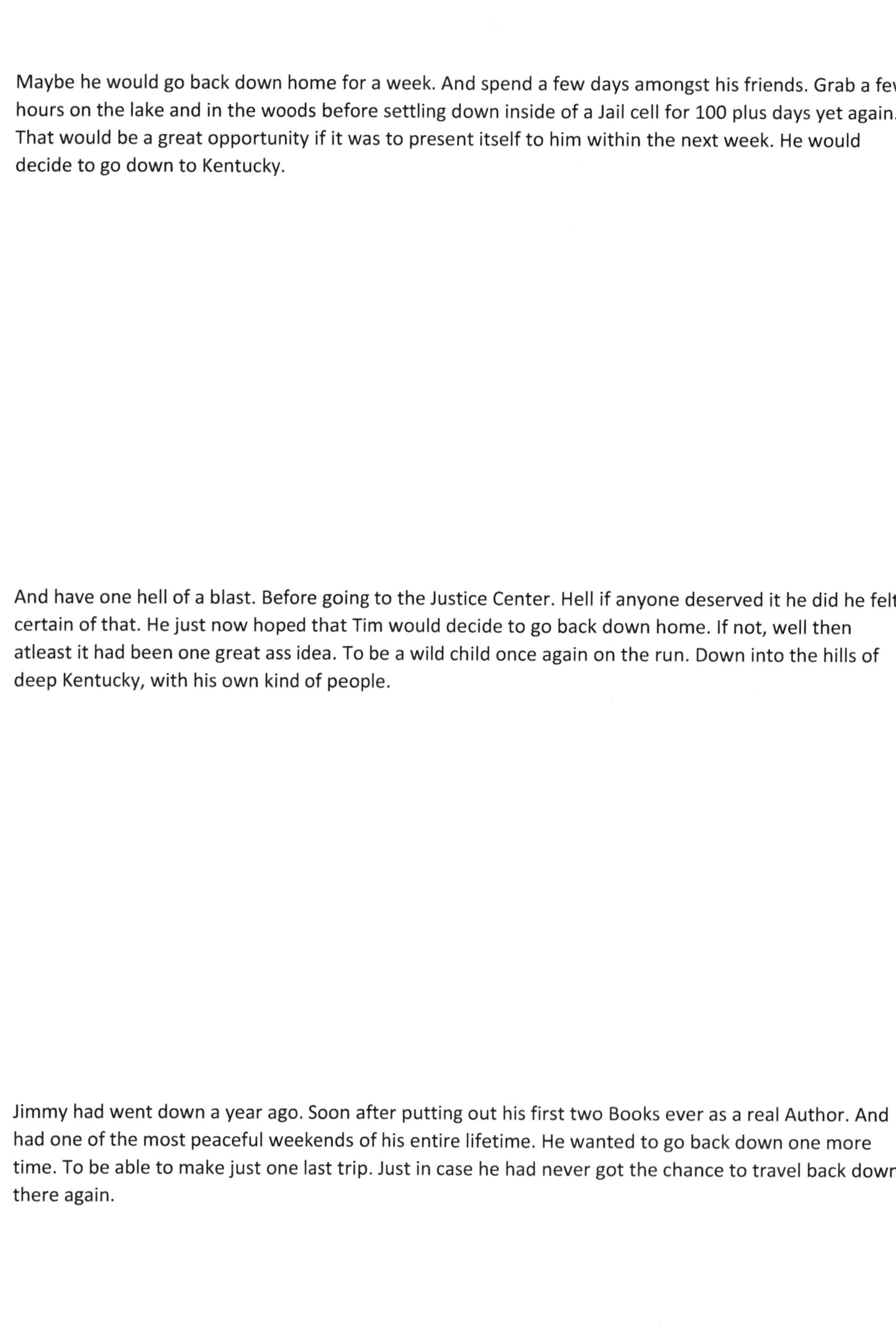

Maybe he would go back down home for a week. And spend a few days amongst his friends. Grab a few hours on the lake and in the woods before settling down inside of a Jail cell for 100 plus days yet again. That would be a great opportunity if it was to present itself to him within the next week. He would decide to go down to Kentucky.

And have one hell of a blast. Before going to the Justice Center. Hell if anyone deserved it he did he felt certain of that. He just now hoped that Tim would decide to go back down home. If not, well then atleast it had been one great ass idea. To be a wild child once again on the run. Down into the hills of deep Kentucky, with his own kind of people.

Jimmy had went down a year ago. Soon after putting out his first two Books ever as a real Author. And had one of the most peaceful weekends of his entire lifetime. He wanted to go back down one more time. To be able to make just one last trip. Just in case he had never got the chance to travel back down there again.

Life up to this point had basically gone to shit for him. Jimmy and his life was now held in the hands of thee most brutal female Judge he had ever come face to face with. His ex wife was thee ex wife from hell. And she was most definetly out to get him. And had been for years now. Thriving off of his down falls and hard times. She really enjoyed seeing the man suffer that was a known fact.

(Chapter 29)

The fact was that she was a deeply troubled woman. Who had harmed herself over time. For not getting what she had wanted. Then soon after her arrive had went to hell. She would end up with several men along her journey. That would control her and beat her as well. Her life becoming total Chaos and Mayhem along the way. She would later blame Jimmy for her bad decisions.

And Jimmy would be the reason for all of it taking place. She had blamed him for everything that had gone wrong in her life. Jimmy knew for a fact that he had no part of the bad happenings going on in her own life. He knew that he had no part in any of it. Her choices were hers. So it was her price to pay. For the bad choices that she had made, not him.

So Jimmy figured that he would probably live the rest of his life. Having an ex wife on his ass. Every single chance she got. For the actions he had made as a young man. Trying to achieve Payback for her being an unfaithful wife during their marriage. Their relationship had mostly been a purely sexual one. They had met very young. And definetly in their early sexual escapades in life.

They would fall for each other. But it was easy to say that it was purely puppy love. That had driven them to their early marriage. During the younger years of their life. Having two children only a year apart from one another would keep the two of them together for the most part. But after only a couple of years. They would both change very quickly.

And want to go down their own paths in life. They would most definetly end up with other people. Simply just to young to be married in the first place. At the age of only 16, wanting to start a life together as a young family. Living the American dream. The house and the White picket fence. With the new car sitting in the driveway.

(Chapter 30)

Jimmy really had messed his whole life up getting married at the age of 16 years old. Still a child in all opinions of the matter. While still in class AA of The Norwood Knothole League. As he played his last

game The Championship Game. The team had lost that game by just one run. It had upset the whole team. In fact so badly.

A heavy night of drinking would occur soon after the game had ended. Several of the players had went over and stayed at their coaches house. They were with his son several of them had decided to drink. In order to sulk over losing the big game. It was a total heart breaker to say the very least. A simple pop fly had been dropped. And just like that the game was over. We had lost the Championship game.

Life would soon change the very next night. As Virginity would be lost by two young lovers. Trying to express their love for one another. After that the lives that would be affected by their uniting together. Would cause major issues among both of their families. Even leading to no contact between family members for well over a year straight. And had caused deep pain for their family members.

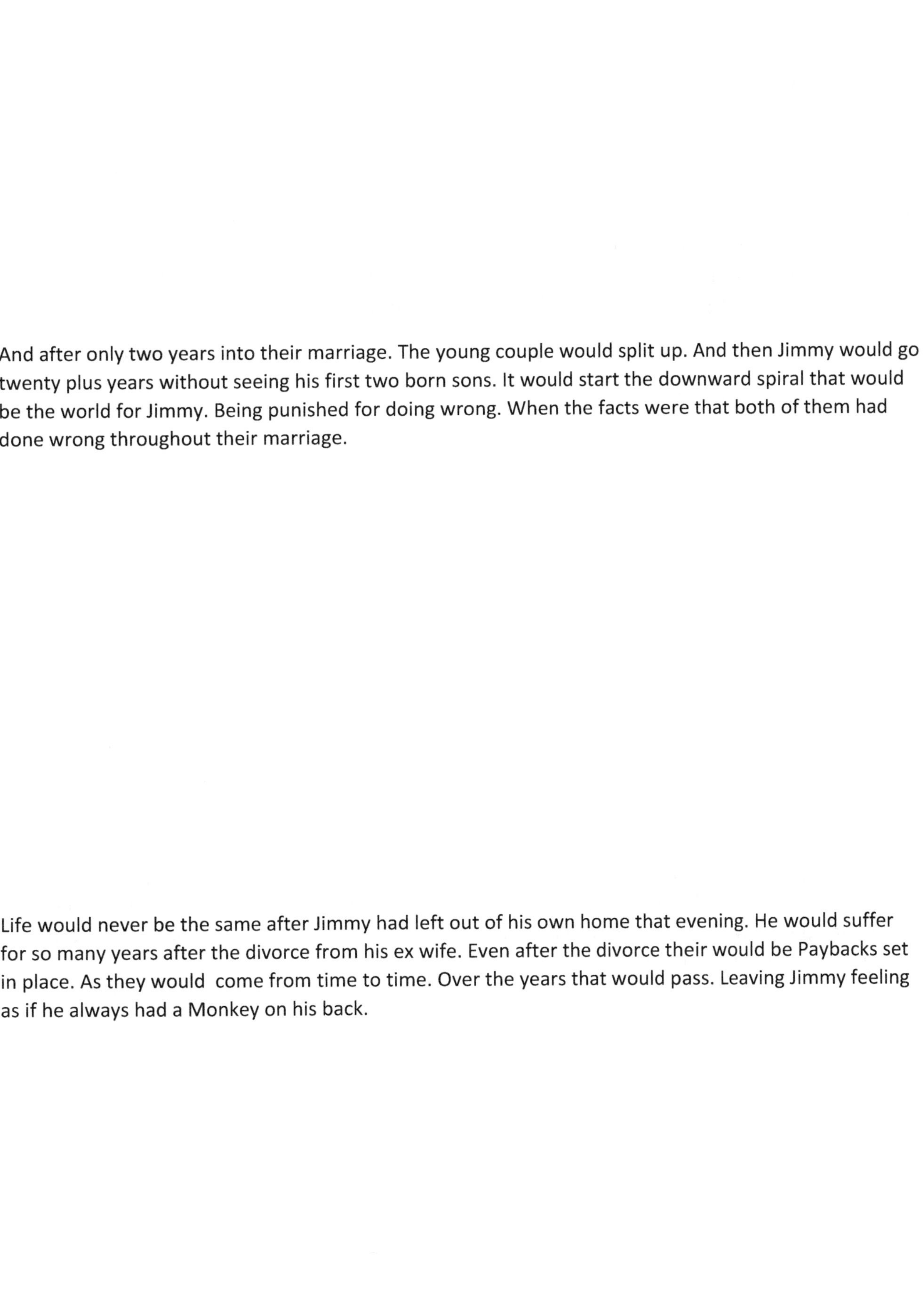

And after only two years into their marriage. The young couple would split up. And then Jimmy would go twenty plus years without seeing his first two born sons. It would start the downward spiral that would be the world for Jimmy. Being punished for doing wrong. When the facts were that both of them had done wrong throughout their marriage.

Life would never be the same after Jimmy had left out of his own home that evening. He would suffer for so many years after the divorce from his ex wife. Even after the divorce their would be Paybacks set in place. As they would come from time to time. Over the years that would pass. Leaving Jimmy feeling as if he always had a Monkey on his back.

The main purpose was to never allow him to live a normal and peaceful life. Always pushing to lock him up in Jail yet once again. That was the one thing that could be done to ruin his livelihood. And it would he sought out every single chance that was presented. For Jimmy the hate that the world carried was just to much to bare any longer. He wanted peace and serenity.

(Chapter 31)

The life of Addiction and Alcoholism had brought forth a maniac. A wild child that was filled with hate. And consumed by every single mistake he had committed in his life. Their had also been very many regrets along the way. The year was now 2022 and the world had completely changed for the worst. Everyone seemed to be losing loved ones.

The pain had become almost to much to bare anymore. Covid had taken so very many lives of the ones that we loved. And we are now facing all out possible War with other countries. What happened to our world we live in. Everything has been changed for the worse. How are human beings supposed to stay strong and united as a country.

With all of this hate running around in it. People need to wake up and smell the coffee. Before it is to late. And there is nothing left that we can do to save our beautiful earth. We need more love spread about and less hate for each other. While we still have a chance to make this world a better place. For our kids and our Grand kids.

We have to get more programs out to help recovering addicts. And we also have to start programs to help those who are coming out of prisons and Jail. To give them a better chance of success. We are failing our people, while we step up and take our help to others elsewhere in the world. While we leave our own people to suffer. The people of our own Country.

While we leave our own on the streets. Something is really wrong about that situation. We have to step up now and help our people of the United States Of America. The time is now not later. We have Waite to long already as it is. While a blind eye is turned. We cannot allow that kind of behavior anymore.

The End

(Written By Jeffrey Lilly)

(August 23rd 2022)

I dedicate this Book to any father out there in the world. Who has gone through a bitter divorce with a significant other. And in the end having their Children kept from them. I feel your pain. For I have been through it myself. All we have at the end, is pure strength and sheer will power to endure life's tests.

www.ingramcontent.com/pod-product-compliance
Lightning Source LLC
LaVergne TN
LVHW080556160826
845677LV00010B/1871

* 9 7 9 8 8 4 8 1 7 4 4 2 7 *